ESSENES

The Elect of Israel and The Priests of Artemis

Allen H. Jones

UNIVERSITY
PRESS OF
AMERICA

LANHAM • NEW YORK • LONDON

Copyright © 1985 by

University Press of America,® Inc.

4720 Boston Way
Lanham, MD 20706

3 Henrietta Street
London WC2E 8LU England

All rights reserved

Printed in the United States of America

Library of Congress Cataloging in Publication Data

Jones, Allen H.
  Essenes: the elect of Israel and the priests of
Artemis.

  Includes index.
  1. Essenes. 2. Artemis (Greek deity) I. Title.
BM175.E8J65 1985   296.8'1   85-9169
ISBN 0-8191-4744-3 (alk. paper)
ISBN 0-8191-4745-1 (pbk. : alk. paper)

All University Press of America books are produced on acid-free
paper which exceeds the minimum standards set by the National
Historical Publications and Records Commission.

VIRGINIA

MY WIFE, MY BEST FRIEND, AND MY BEST GIRL

ACKNOWLEDGEMENTS

No one, of course has written a book of this type without the help of many.

My deep gratitude goes to Cyrus H. Gordon, Professor of Hebraic Studies and Director of the Center for Ebla Studies at New York University. Dr. Gordon and I have been friends for thirty-odd years, and he has never failed to give me help and counsel whenever I have made the request.

After retirement, I moved to Hilton Head, South Carolina, where the opportunities for study and research are hardly what they are in the Washington, D.C area, where I had lived for thirty years. But the people here have helped to offset this handicap. While the library here is small, the librarians have on occasion been able to procure for me material not ordinarily accessible. The library and the librarians at the University of South Carolina at Columbia, were also most gracious and willing to assist. Dr. William O. Nisbet, minister of the First Presbyterian Church was also most kind in being willing to discuss some particular aspect of the subject and to offer me use of some of his reference works. I consulted with Mr. Howard Germaine on some linguistic problems of Hebrew. Manuel and Olive Holland deserve my warm thanks for their allowing me to use their office facilities in the preparation of the manuscript. Kathy Edwards has been most helpful with many suggestions. Even the United States Senator from South Carolina, the Honorable Strom Thurmond, helped in enlisting the resources of the Library of Congress during my visits there. In other words, thanks, neighbors!

I would be most remiss if I neglected to mention an old friend and former student of mine, Gordon Campbell of Rockville, Maryland, a member of the Maryland-National Capital Park and Planning Commission, who most willingly and ably prepared the maps for this book.

TABLE OF CONTENTS

PREFACE

The unearthing of the celebrated Dead Sea Scrolls was one of the most important discoveries of its kind in history, and public interest in both the Scrolls and the sect which produced them has not seemed to diminish. There is <u>almost</u> universal agreement that the group responsible was a sect of the Jews known as "Essenes" by other Jews and Gentiles, if not by themselves. This most devout of the Jewish sects thought of, and referred to, themselves as the "Elect" of their God.

At the same time in history, the goddess Artemis was still being worshipped in the East Mediterranean area, whose temple, to become considered as one of the Seven Wonders of the World, was located at Ephesus on the coast of Asia Minor. Indeed, Artemis-worship was so firmly established that it was a strong rival of both Judaism and early Christianity. One set of priests ministering to the goddess at Ephesus was also known by the term "Essenes." The question immediately becomes apparent as to what relationship, if any, existed between the Jewish Essenes and the Artemisian Essenes. Scholars seem to have remained skeptical of any connection, at least up to this point.

The writing of this book was not easy. Aside from my proclivity to be easily enticed into some outdoor activity, there remained the more serious difficulty that scholars have never been in any general agreement as to the etymology of <u>Essene</u>. The one suggested in the text has been considered by some but then rejected. This rejection, however, was based upon a lack of consideration of one aspect. This added consideration leads us to a possible relationship between the two groups.

Another difficulty results from prejudices which exist against any sort of suggestion of a possible relationship between pagan worship and the worship of the Judeo-Christian God. Yet geographically the Jews and early Christians were neighbors of people who had worshipped Artemis for many centuries - before the emergence of the Hebrews as a nation. Also it was Ephesus itself from which St. Paul worked, and one of his letters was addressed to the early Christians at that city.

These were not the only difficulties, of course.

The question as to how much material to include was a most bothersome one. It might seem to some that discussion of the early Greeks (or Mycenaeans or Hellenes, whichever name you prefer) and their gods along with the early Minoan culture, might be far afield from a consideration of a relatively obscure Jewish sect, the Essenes, which came into existence at a much later date, at least by that name. Yet it seems from this vantage point that relationships between the peoples involved remain obscure and cloudy, except to some scholars, unless some aspects of historical perspective are developed. It is perhaps ironic that such relatively small groups as the two sets of Essenes should require such a broad perspective.

Hilton Head
South Carolina
1985

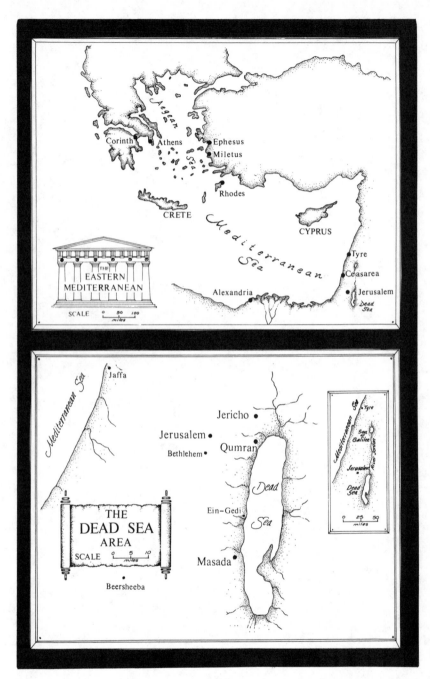

THE EASTERN MEDITERRANEAN

Corinth · Athens · Ephesus · Miletus · Rhodes · CRETE · CYPRUS · Tyre · Ceasarea · Alexandria · Jerusalem

SCALE 0 50 100 miles

THE DEAD SEA AREA

Jaffa · Jericho · Jerusalem · Bethlehem · Qumran · Ein-Gedi · Masada · Beersheeba

Dead Sea

SCALE 0 5 10 miles

CHAPTER I

THE ESSENES

Since the discovery in 1947 of the so-called Dead Sea Scrolls at Qumran in Israel, thousands of books and articles have been published concerning what is undoubtedly one of the most significant discoveries of all time. A. Dupont-Sommer, commenting on the vast bibliography, indicated that even by the beginning of 1957 there had been a bibliography compiled by a German scholar, A. Burchard, listing 1538 titles, omitting writings of a popular type. Dupont-Sommer adds that in fact a word has been coined in Germany, Qumranology.[1] I have seen no figures compiled since that date, but interest in the Scrolls has never seemed to diminish.

Much of this writing of course has had to do with the contents of the Scrolls, but much also concerned the sect that produced them. The members had apparently occupied a monastery at Qumran near the northwest corner of the Dead Sea, where they followed their way of life. The popular picture is one of peaceful ascetics living a monastic existence cut off from the rest of the world, but as will be seen, this picture is somewhat distorted. Some of the community were scribes who spent their time in the scriptorium, writing or copying from previous manuscripts what they considered to be the heart of Judaism. Then from evidence it is obvious that the monastery had been destroyed by fire, probably during the war with Rome which resulted in the destruction of Jerusalem in 70 AD. and the fortress of Masada in 73 AD. Such a fate had been anticipated by the community, and members had placed their precious Scrolls in jars and took them to the more inaccessible of the many caves which permeate the area. How inaccessible these caves were (and are) is attested by the fact that when none of the sect apparently ever returned, the Scrolls remained undiscovered until the middle of the twentieth century.

It did not take scholars long to attribute these ancient writings to a Jewish sect known as "Essenes." The late Professor Sukenik of the Hebrew University in Jerusalem was the first to identify the sect of

1

the Scrolls as Essenes, and today this identification is almost universally accepted. Nevertheless, it has been necessary on occasion for us to be reminded that strictly speaking we don't know who wrote the Scrolls, because while the Qumran community called itself by many names, "Essenes" was not one. In fact, this name does not appear in either the Old or the New Testament. The Qumran group referred to itself as the "Elect," or the "Elect of God," the "Poor," "God's Plantation," "Sons of Light." The community also thought of itself as the "Remnant," constituting the true "relic" of Israel. The important implication as seen in these titles is that the Qumran community regarded itself as something special, the members being enlightened to the Truth as opposed to those who deviated from the Truth and therefore walked in Darkness. They indeed thought of themselves as the true priests of God. The above titles have been translated thus by Theodor Gaster in his <u>Dead Sea Scriptures</u>, who notes that these same titles are found elsewhere, in both the Old and the New Testaments, as well as in the writings of other peoples.² But no "Essenes." Apart from the Scrolls themselves, we get acquainted with the community through people who wrote in a language other than Hebrew or Aramaic. Flavius Josephus, Philo of Alexandria, and Pliny the Elder are the main sources of information, while later writers such as Hippolytus, Eusebius, and Porphyry also made some contributions to our knowledge of the Essenes.

At this point it should be explained that the initial finds at Qumran set off searches for scrolls throughout the area, some of which were fruitful, In addition to the eleven caves at Qumran, four other sites yielded ancient scrolls. Since the Qumran documents had already been given the name "Dead Sea Scrolls," subsequently the tendency was to include the scrolls from the other sites under that name. But in this study, when reference is made to the Dead Sea Scrolls, only those from Qumran are meant-with two exceptions. One of these exceptions is a fragment of a scroll found during the excavations at the fortress of Masada, about thirty miles below Qumran on the shore of the Dead Sea. This scroll is most important and will be referred to later. The second exception is what is known as the <u>Damascus Scroll</u> or the <u>Zadokite Fragments</u>. This Hebrew document was found among other manuscripts in the <u>Geniza</u> of a synagogue in old Cairo in 1896-7 and published in 1910. It was given a great deal of study at the time but little agreement was reached. All that was clear was that members of the organization called themselves the "Sons of Zadok," and their organization "The New Covenant in the Land of Damascus." Then in 1948 several fragments were found at Qumran, and with study, it became clear that the sect which produced the Dead$_3$ Sea Scrolls had also produced the Zadokite Document.[3] Because of the weight of evidence, this sect will be referred to as Essenes.

But the term "Essene" has remained a mystery. There have been suggestions that the name might well be an epithet, perhaps born of derision by those who were ridiculing the members of the group for some reason, and then after a period of time the original meaning may have been forgotten in admiration of their high moral principles, in the same way that the original meaning of "Quakers" has been forgotten. Duncan Howlett is one who has made this suggestion. He reminds us that in the Graeco-Roman period, the opponents of the party receptive to Hellenizing influence became known as Pharisees, meaning "Separators," an obvious epithet. He further suggests that in the same way, a branch of the Pharisees believed that they were forced to make a choice between what they considered strict adherence to the Law and deviation from it, this branch becoming the Essenes.[4] But even after considering the possibility that "Essenes" may be an epithet, many questions about them still remain unanswered.

It is obvious from the lists in the bibliographies that the focus of attention has been, rightly so, on the Scrolls themselves - on their translation, analysis, and what they reveal as an evolutionary link between Judaism and Christianity. But because there is no reference to "Essenes" in the Scrolls themselves and so few references by others, little has been able to be said about the group's history and its relationships to other groups and cultures in that geographical area. And as might be expected, much of what has been said remains open to question.

Let us consider first the four main sources of information concerning the Essenes: Pliny the Elder, Philo of Alexandria, Flavius Josephus, and St. Hippolytus of Rome.

Pliny the Elder (23-79 AD.), a Roman of equestrian

3

rank, was at one time a fellow-soldier of Vespasian, the conqueror of Palestine, and probably spent some time in that country. In his Naturalis Historia he includes a topographical description of Palestine, which seems to be accurate. This section includes his reference to the "lone tribe" of Essenes, and his decription of the site of their abode fits that of Khirbet Qumran.[5] This is a significant bit of evidence that those of the Qumran community were indeed Essenes.

Philo (c.20 BC.-?) was a famous Jewish philosopher who lived in Alexandria and spent the greater part of his life there. He wrote in Greek and was what the editors of the Loeb Classical Library Edition call "the most important example of the Hellenized Jews outside of Palestine." Perhaps he became knowledgeable of the Essenes when he took a trip to Jerusalem during his youth. But also he knew a group in Egypt, the Theraputae, who in some ways resembled the Essenes.

The third and probably the most reliable source is Flavius Josephus (37-97 AD.), a Jew born in Jerusalem of a distinguished family. He made himself learned in Jewish law and Greek literature and wrote his histories in Greek. He was also a noted soldier and took a short part in the Jewish war against Rome. It is not the purpose here to pass judgment on his defection to Rome. Rather, the significant point is, if we can believe his autobiographical comments, he had studied the requirements of the three sects, the Sadducees, the Pharisees, and the Essenes, for the purpose of joining one. Whether the Essenes were too rigorous in their expectations of the applicant, we do not know. But Josephus joined the Pharisees. Nevertheless, his knowledge of the Essenes had to be much more extensive than that of the others. One of his accounts of the Essenes is contained in his Jewish War and the other in his Jewish Antiquities, and if a few inconsistencies are apparent, one should be reminded of the fraility of the human memory, for these two works were written twenty years apart.

The fourth source, St. Hippolytus of Rome (170-236 AD.), was an early Church Father. His Refutation of All Heresies, while including an account of the Essenes, is not usually considered a major source of information about them. He lived somewhat later than the others, and his account closely parallels that of Josephus. However, it is believed by many that he is not repeating Josephus, but both might have been using a common source. If so, this could account for both the similarities and the differences, and what is more important, it could offset some of the natural biases to which Josephus was subjected. Moreover, there is some important information contained in Hippolytus alone.

What do these sources have to say about the Essenes? About their history, very little, although some information which they do give will be referred to at the appropriate time. Their chief contributions had to do with the activities of the Essenes during the Roman period. But one matter on which they all agreed was the extremely high moral character of the members of the community.

With so much attention being centered upon the Essenes at Qumran, one might gain the impression that this group comprised the entire sect, that they had removed themselves from society to live a monastic and ascetic life in their settlement by the Dead Sea. Such an impression would be erroneous, for the weight of evidence has them dispersed throughout Judea. It is true that Pliny the Elder limited the Essenes to a single tribe (gens sola) and described their living at what is undoubtedly the site of Khirbet Qumran.[6] But Philo, Josephus, and Hippolytus all contradict Pliny's statement that the Essenes were a single tribe living at one place. Philo, in his Every Good Man Is Free maintained that they lived in villages, although apparently avoiding the cities as "places of iniquity" which would have a "deadly effect upon their own souls."[7] Elsewhere, in his Hypothetica, Philo states that the Essenes "live in many cities of Judea and in many villages and grouped in great societies of many numbers."[8] This portion of the Hypothetica we owe to Eusebius, who reported it many years later, which may account for the contradiction about their living in cities, but the important point is that according to Philo, the Essenes lived in settlements, whether cities, villages, or both, throughout Judea.

Josephus agrees that the Essenes lived in villages and cities, but adds that some were in the habit of traveling. He states that "they occupy no one city but settle in large numbers in every town. On the arrival of any of the sect from elsewhere, all the resources of the community are put at their disposal, just as if they were their own....In every city there is one of their order expressly appointed to attend to strangers, who provides them with raiment and other necessaries."9 From this it can be assumed that the Essenes lived in colonies in the towns and cities throughout Judea. This is not to deny, however, that they also had their own settlements, such as the one at Qumran, which might even have been a head-quarters.

Life within these communities was rigorous and well-ordered. At one point Josephus informs his readers that the sole occupation of the Essenes was agricultural labor,[10] but in his earlier work, The Jewish War, he gives a different impression, noting that even before breakfast the Essenes "were dismissed by their superiors to the various crafts in which they were severally proficient and are strenu-ously employed until the fifth hour." Then after purification by water, they assembled in the refectory for their meal, after which they returned to their respective crafts.[11] This passage does not convey the impression that the Essenes were limited to agricu-ltural labors.

Philo, in his Hypothetica, also stated that the Essenes had various occupations at which they worked from sun-up to sun-down. While some farmed, he reported, others were herdsmen, and some attended swarms of bees (this occupation will be referred to later as it is of some significance). Still others, he continued, worked at the handicrafts that were needed to make the community self-sufficient, and "they shrink from no innocent way of getting a live-lihood."[12] Thus it may safely be assumed that while a portion of the work done by the members of the community was agricultural, there were other kinds of work which had to be performed for their everyday living.

A day in the life of the members pictures the austerity and piety practiced by the Essenes. Josephus relates that they were up before sunrise, during which time no word on "mundane affairs" was spoken. They then offered to the sun, Josephus claims, certain prayers which had been handed down from their fore-fathers, as though"they were entreating the sun to rise.[13] Such a practice seems quite unJewish, and some scholars including the scholiast for Josephus,

6

have attempted to rationalize this ritual.[14] But it will be shown later that this practice was followed by the followers of Pythagoreanism and that this philosophy was followed to at least some extent by the Essenes.

Following their prayers to the sun, Josephus continues, they were dismissed by their superiors to perform their various tasks until the fifth hour, at which time they again assembled, girded their loins with linen cloths and bathed their bodies as a purification in cold water. They then assembled again in a place which apparently in some way was considered holy, for the uninitiated were not allowed to enter. Now considered pure, they went to the refectory, where they took their seats in silence. The baker then served rolls to them in order, and the cook set before each a plate with a single course, but none was permitted to partake until the priest had said a grace. Another grace was said at the end of the meal, after which they laid aside their raiment, as "holy vestments," and returned to their labor until evening. They made their evening meal in the same way, but any guests who might have arrived during the day sat with them. Josephus adds that "No clamor or disturbance ever pollutes their dwelling; they speak in turn, each making way for his neighbor."[15]

All the above details suggest a communal type life, which indeed it was. Philo, too, relates in his Every Good Man Is Free how a community of Essenes held all goods all goods in common: house, clothes, food, wages -everything. Wages were held in a single treasury from which all disbursements were made to those who might need to use them. Furthermore, adds Philo, the sick were taken care of and the cost of their treatment came from the common stock. The elderly, too, were cared for and "receive from countless hands and minds a full and generous maintenance for their latter years."[16] In his Hypothetica Philo concludes: "Thus having each day a common life and common table they are content with the same conditions, lovers of frugality who shun expensive luxury as a disease of both body and soul."[17]

Josephus, both in his Antiquities and War commented about the communal life of the Essenes. In the former, he merely notes that the Essenes held their possessions in common, and the "wealthy man

7

receives no more enjoyment from his property than the man who posseses nothing."[18] In his <u>War</u> he discusses the Essenes' communal living at greater length, explaining the method by which all the members of the community were given financial equality. He claims that the Essenes had a law which required the Order to confiscate the property of the new members, and thus all, like brothers, enjoyed a single patrimony. Once in the Order, the members were not allowed to buy or sell, everyone receiving what he needed, whether or not he could make any return.[19]

An outstanding quality of the Essenes' way of life was a strict sense of justice. The group, for example, had an extremely enlightened view concerning slavery - enlightened even for today, and most certainly for those times. Philo in his <u>Every Good Man Is Free</u>, has the following to say about the Essenes: "Not a slave is to be found among them, but all are free, exchanging services with each other, and they denounce the owners of slaves, not merely for their injustice in outraging the laws of equality, but also for their impiety in annulling the statute of Nature, who mother-like has born and reared all men alike, not in mere name but in reality..."[20] Are not these words reminiscent of those of Thomas Jefferson 1800 years later?

Josephus also refers to the conviction of the Essenes concerning slavery. He states that the Essenes did not own slaves, for it was their belief that the practice of slavery contributes to injustice.[21] This concept was a radical departure from what at the time was a universal institution - even the Hebrews participating - and shows that the Essenes followed the highest concepts of social justice as preached earlier by the Hebrew prophets.

But in the matter of women and marriage, the Essenes did not seem to be so enlightened, judging by present-day trends. Marriage and the company of women the Essenes shunned, at least for the most part (an exception will be noted later). In his short reference to the Essenes, Pliny seems to be much impressed by this curious social phenomenon. He called the Essenes a "...tribe remarkable beyond all the other tribes in the whole world, as it has no women and has renounced all sexual desire."[22] It is noteworthy that impressed as he most certainly was, Pliny refrained from any editorial comments.

8

Philo, however, felt no such restraint. After
stating that the Essenes eschewed marriage, he listed
the reasons for the celibacy of the members, which
added up to a diatribe against wives. A wife, asserts
Philo, is selfish, jealous, and adept at beguiling
the morals of her husband. Moreover, he continues,
she practices her arts as an actress on the stage,
first ensnaring the husband's senses and finally
his mind. Philo's conclusion is that he who puts
his wife and children first - as the result of her
arts and practices - ceases to be the same to others,
becoming a different man and passing from freedom
into slavery. The scholiast believes that these
remarks should not be taken as Philo's own opinion
but reflected what the Essenes thought.[23] This may
be the case, but Philo does not make clear the distinction.

In both his War and Antiquities Josephus also
comments on the celibacy of the Essenes. In the
latter he merely states matter-of-factly that the
Essenes brought no wives into the community, for
they were a source of dissension,[24] a remark echoing
the statements by Philo. But in his War, Josephus
has some interesting variations. While still maintaining that the Essenes disdained marriage, he added
that they adopted the children of other men,[25] information that neither Pliny nor Philo reveal. But
the Jewish historian goes even further. In this
same account, he tells of one Order of Essenes who
practiced marriage. He relates how the members of
this particular order of Essenes believed that those
who do not marry cut off their chief function of
life: the propagation of the race. But these members
of the Essenes were not allowed to enter into marriage
lightly, for Josephus goes on to say that a three-
year probation for the wives was required.[26] As might
be expected, this passage is a bit ambiguous and
the details do not come through clearly.

Excavations at Qumran have given support to
Josephus's assertion that some Essenes had wives
and children. Although the main cemetery there has
yielded only male skeletons, at least until this
time, skeletons of women and children have been found
in the secondary burial grounds. There has been
speculation as to whether only certain orders permitted
marriage. But the important point, nevertheless,
is that the Essenes placed strong emphasis upon the
celibacy of its members.

How did an aspiring young Jew become a member of the Essenes? It was not an easy undertaking. Josephus once remarked that he had once submitted himself to the rigorous training for the sect, but finally became a Pharisee. It is easy for one who holds the character of Josephus in low esteem to believe that the Essenic training was too demanding of him, but perhaps that is judging too harshly. At any rate, he informs us that an applicant for the Order was not immediately admitted but must pass through four grades.[28] First, there was a probationary period of one year, during which time he remained "outside the fraternity" but given the Order's "rule of life." If he gave proof of his temperance during that year, he was brought into closer touch with the community and allowed to "share the purer kind of holy water" but was not yet allowed to attend meetings. Following this, his character was tested for two more years, and only then, if found worthy, was he enrolled in the Society.[29] The Manual of Discipline, the Qumran scroll which prescribed the rules of the Order, is in general agreement with Josephus.

But while Josephus and the Manual of Discipline are in general agreement, both the Manual and the Zadokite Document vary somewhat from the account of Josephus. Referring to these two Scrolls, Gaster points out that children had to undergo a ten-year period of study from a manual called the Book of Study, and when twenty years of age, they could present themselves for membership. At this point the applicants were publicly examined for both moral and intellectual character, and if approved, they were admitted for a year's probation, during which time they could not share in the community's resources, nor were they admitted to the common table. If their behavior during this year of probation was satisfactory, they were admitted to another year of probation, this time within the community, and they were required to place all their property in trust with an overseer. At the end of this second year, they were fully enrolled if the vote was favorable and after swearing the oath of allegiance. At that time he was listed in an order of rank, which was reviewed from year to year, promotions or demotions being determined by general vote.[30]

This oath of allegiance is also mentioned by Josephus, as well as by Pliny and Hippolytus, but Philo's account differs in some respects. Josephus, for example, at one point maintained that the Essenes swore no oaths,[31] that their word carried more force than any oath,[31] while Philo merely states that the Essenes refrained from oaths.[32] It is realized that the difference here between them is not substantial, but the swearing of "tremendous oaths," as Josephus put it, seems out of place in an Order which banned all oaths. At any rate, if oaths were banned, the oath of allegiance was an exception to the rule.

Josephus has written down this oath of allegiance and it may be instructive to reproduce is as Josephus has recorded it, for it gives us great insight into the character of the Essenes:

> he will wrong none, whether of his own volition or on the orders of another;
>
> he will forever hate the unjust and fight the battle of the just;
>
> he will keep faith with all men, especially with the powers that be, since no ruler attains his office save by the will of God;
>
> should he himself bear rule, he will never abuse his authority nor, either in dress or by other outward marks of superiority, outshine his subjects;
>
> he will forever be a lover of the truth and will expose liars;
>
> he will keep his hands from stealing and his soul pure from unholy gain;
>
> he will conceal nothing from the members of the sect and will report none of their secrets to others, even though tortured to death;
>
> he will transmit the rules exactly as he himself received them;
>
> he will abstain from robbery;
>
> he will carefully preserve the books of the sect and the names of the angels.[33]

11

Today we undoubtedly owe the existence of these Scrolls to this last vow, and as we shall see, others of these bear directly upon our subject and will give us greater understanding of the actions of the group.

But if these were indeed what the novices swore to before being admitted to the Order, it seems strange that Josephus, if he is writing from first-hand knowledge, should reveal the oath because revelation of the Order's secrets to those outside the Order violated the oath.[34] It is possible, however, that this was not first-hand knowledge, for Hippolytus repeats the same oath. Whether Hippolytus was merely repeating Josephus, or whether they both used a common source is difficult to say.

Three matters concerning the oath are worthy of particular note. The first has to do with the organization of the community. Several of the vows imply that the Essenes were a highly structured society. The individual Essene did nothing without orders from his superior. Two things only, adds Josephus, are left to individual discretion: the rendering of assistance and compassion,[35] a statement that speaks volumes. The historian then felt a need to qualify his assertion, for he added that the assistance had to be for those in need - presents to relatives, for example,[36] were prohibited without leave from the "managers." Even when they went to the synagogue, Philo relates, the members were arranged in rows according to their age, the younger below the elder. This strict hierarchal system was made clear by both Josephus and Philo.

Millar Burrows succinctly describes the higher echelons of the Order and perhaps it would be well to reproduce two paragraphs from his <u>More Light on the Dead Sea Scrolls</u>. Before doing so, however, it is necessary to say a short word about the term <u>Messiah</u>, since it is used in Burrow's passage. The word is really a title meaning "Anointed," and in Greek it is rendered <u>Xristos</u>. But these "Anointed Ones" of Israel were not thought of as saviors, as Xristos, or Christ, was thought of in later Christian theology. As will be seen, the Essenes, as well as the other Jewish sects, believed in two messiahs: a priestly messiah of the House of Aaron, and a royal messiah of the House of David, presiding over their ideal and divinely-willed socioreligious Order. And so the two paragraphs from Burrows:

12

"As there was a priestly and a lay Messiah, so the sect consited of two main divisions, the priests and the Levites and the laity. The priests were called sons Of Aaron and sons of Zadok; it was they who ruled, and one of them had to meet with every group of ten members. The assembly of fully-initiated members had considerable administrative authority, especially in matters of admission and discipline, but the ultimate power, both legislative and judicial, seems to have been reserved for the priests. Milik (J.T., noted Scrolls authority) finds the same division between priestly and lay authority in the Damascus Document (Zadokite Document). The 'superintendent who is over all the camps' is a layman, whose function is administrative; the 'priest who is appointed at the head of the many' has the re-ligious function of teaching the law. There is also a 'superintendent of the camp' who teaches sacred history and exercises a pastoral oversight which seems to imply that he is a priest.

"At the head of the community, according to the Manual of Discipline, there is a council of twelve laymen and three priests. Milik may be right in suggesting that the twelve laymen represent the twelve tribes of Israel and the three priests represent the priestly families of Gershom, Kohath, and Merari, the three sons of Levi, though the priesthood was actually limited to the descendents of Aaron, the grandson of Kohath. Instead of the council of twelve, the Damascus Document prescribes ten judges, of whom four are priests 'of the tribe of Levi and Aaron' and six are laymen 'from Israel.'"[38]

Thus Burrows describes the higher echelons of the Order.

The second matter of note is related to the first. The discipline regarding obedience to su-periors applied not only to those within the sect, but extended as well to the Jewish rulers. The third vow makes this clear. The Essenes were bound by oath to support loyally the rulers of Israel. For some time, this meant the Hasmoneans, and with them this support and obedience came hard at times, but when Herod came to the throne, the situation became intolerable because Herod had usurped the office.

The third matter of interest in the oath sworn by

the neophyte is the vow that "he will forever hate the unjust and fight the battle of the just." Such a vow is incongruous to the popular picture of the Essenes leading a peaceful and ascetic life. Philo is at least partially responsible for the misleading popular picture of the Essenes when he states in his Every Good Man Is Free "As for darts, javelins, daggers, or the helmet, breastplate or shield, you could not find a single manufacturer of them, nor, in general, any person making weapons or plying any industry concerned with war...." 39 This description by Philo of the Essenes as pacifistic does not seem to fit a group who have vowed to hate evil and to fight the battle of the just. Perhaps since he lived in Alexandria, Philo was thinking of a group in Egypt, often compared to the Essenes, the Theraputae.

Josephus differs sharply with the statement by Philo. In relating how individual Essenes traveled from place to place, the historian notes that they carried arms as a protection against brigands.[40] Traveling at that time was of course quite hazardous because of highwaymen (recall the parable of the Good Samaritan), and to the Essenes, as noted in their oath, robbery was especially heinous and also unjust. Thus for the Essenes, carrying arms on a journey was not only practical as a means for self-preservation, but at the same time they were fulfilling their oath to fight the battle of the just. Josephus also describes the physical courage of the Essenes during the war with Rome, a part which deserves more space later. The Essenes, then, while ordinarily peaceful in their daily life, were capable on occasion of violence and, as we shall see, fighting fanatically.

Here is a sect, then, whose members led an austere communal type life, organized in a highly structured hierarchal system. They saw their primary duty as piety toward the Deity and justice toward men, and loyalty to the rulers both of the Order and of Israel, even if the performance of this duty meant violence and death.

NOTES TO CHAPTER I

1. A. Dupont-Sommer, The Essene Writings from Qumran, trans. G. Vermes (Gloucester: Peter Smith, 1973), p. 7-8.

2. Theodor Gaster, The Dead Sea Scriptures (Garden City: Doubleday, 1956), p. 21.

3. Dupont-Sommer, p. 39-40.

4. Duncan Howlett, The Essenes and Christianity (New York: Harper, 1957), p. 51.

5. Pliny, Natural History (Loeb Classical Library Edition, Cambridge: Harvard, 1969), V.73

6. Ibid.

7. Philo, Every Good Man Is Free (Loeb, 1967), 76.

8. Ibid., Hypothetica (Loeb), 7.19-11.1

9. Josephus, The Jewish War (Loeb, 1967), II.126.

10. Ibid., Antiquities of the Jews, XVIII.19.

11. Ibid., War, 129.

12. Philo, Hypothetica, 11.9.

13. Josephus, War, II.128.

14. Ibid.

15. Ibid. War, II.130-133.

16. Philo, Every Good Man Is Free, 86-87.

17. Ibid., Hypothetica 11.11.

18. Josephus, Antiquities XVIII.21.

19. Ibid., War II.122

20. Philo, Every Good Man Is Free, 79.

21. Josephus, Antiquities XVIII.21.

22. Pliny, V.73.

23. Philo, Hypothetica 11.14.

24. Josephus, Antiquities XVIII.21.

25. Ibid.,War II.120.

26. Ibid., 161.

27. Ibid., The Life Against Apion, 1112.

28. Ibid., War, II.150.

29. Ibid., 137-138.

30. Manual of Discipline VI.13-23 as translated by Gaster, p. 9-10.

31. Josephus, War II.135.

32. Philo, Every Good Man Is Free, 84.

33. Josephus, War II.139-142.

34. Hippolytus, The Refutation of All Heresies, ed. The Reverend Alexander Roberts and James Donaldson (Grand Rapids: Erdmans, 1951), Chapter XVIII.

35. Josephus, War II.134.

36. Ibid.

37. Philo, Every Good Man Is Free, 81.

38. Millar Burrows, More Light on the Dead Sea Scrolls (New York: Viking, 1958), p. 245.

39. Philo, Every Good Man Is Free, 78.

40. Josephus, War II.125.

CHAPTER II

RELTIVES AND FOREBEARS OF THE ESSENES

Josephus in his Antiquities claimed that the Jews had three "philosophies," the Pharisees, the Sadducees, and the Essenes. He further claimed that the three went back to the "most ancient times."[1] This is a most amazing statement, for there is a complete lack of evidence that these three sects went back very far into history - at least by those names. The three groups appeared under these names probably about the time of the Maccabean Rebellion in 167 BC., or perhaps during the Hasmonean period from 142 - 63 BC. It is indeed even possible that the rise of the Hasmonean dynasty was responsible in some way for the coming into existence of these sects.

Pliny and Philo ignore the Pharisees and Sadducees but are in complete agreement with Josephus as to the antiquity of the Essenes. Pliny claimed that the Essenes had existed for "thousands of ages," and then appropriately and parenthetically added "incredibile dictu."[2] Philo traces the Essenes back to Moses: "Multitudes of his disciples has the lawgiver trained for the life of fellowship (the lawgiver was probably Moses). These people are called Essenes, a name awarded them doubtless in recognition of their holiness."[3] Thus, in addition to tracing the Essenes back to Moses, Philo suggests that their name comes from the Greek word ostiotes, meaning "holiness." The point here is not whether Philo was correct in his etymology (that will be examined in a later chapter), but that he suspected that that the name Essenes is derived from the Greek rather than from the Hebrew. If so, it would be an item of evidence that the name was taken or bestowed during the Graeco-Roman period.

The Pharisees and the Sadducees, the two other "philosophies" mentioned by Josephus, seem to have adopted their respective names at about the same time as the Essenes received theirs. It would be both confusing and irrelevant to discourse at length on these two sects, but because of certain relationships among the three, a number of matters should be mentioned. Perhaps it would be enlightening to list the chief differences between the Pharisees and the Sadducees as seen by a scholar-clergyman, the late A. Powell Davies:

"...1. The Sadducees charged that the Pharisees taught the people observances that were not written in the law of Moses - which was true in the sense that Mosaic law was interpreted by the Pharisees to meet contemporary conditions;

2. the Pharisees believed in immortality, heaven and hell, a general resurrection, a Messianic kingdom, concerning all of which the Sadducees claimed that nothing should be taught since nothing is known;

3. the Sadducees held the Hellenic doctrine of free will, whereas the Pharisees contended that free will was limited by the predestinate purposes of God;

4. the Pharisees held that the practices of the Sadducees were inconsistent with the obligations of high priesthood - which was conspicuously and painfully true;

5. the Pharisees were proselytizers, believing in an international Jewish community or church, into which all might enter who would accept the Jewish law and the Pharisaic ritual requirements, and were interested chiefly in the Judaism of the synagogue. The Sadducees cared nothing for winning converts, and their interest was the Temple and power centralized at Jerusalem."[4]

Davies adds a footnote explaining that on #5 the Pharisees reversed themselves and withdrew from the missionary program during the early successes of the Christian churches.[5]

It might seem that the above-listed contrasts show clear-cut differences between the Pharisees and the Sadducees, and while these differences are important and helpful to understanding, they sometimes tend to overlap and the picture becomes confused. For example, as noted above, it would depend on the historical date as to whether the Pharisees could be regarded as missionaries or not. In addition, inspite of the statement by Josephus, the Pharisees, Sadducees, and Essenes were not the only sects of Judaism during the Graeco-Roman Age. There were others groups, among them the Hasideans, who played an important role during the Maccabean rebellion. W. R. Farmer believes that the Pharisees and the Essenes developed out of rival wings of the Hasideans,[6] which would account for the many similarities, as well as the differences, between the Pharisees and the Essenes. But does this mean, then, that the Sadducees, on the other hand can be separated entirely from the Essenes in their philosophy, Quite the contrary.

The name Sadducee is derived from "Sadok," or "Zadok," who had been appointed high priest by Solomon in his time and who then became the father of the Jerusalem priesthood, the "sons of Zadok." But in spite of deriving their name from Zadok, the Sadducees, like the Essenes and the other sects, did not come into being as a party until about Maccabean times. One may conclude from this that the Maccabean rebellion and the following Hasmonean period are a focal point for the emergence of the Pharisees, the Essenes, and the Sadducees, the "sons of Zadok." The name "Zadok" and "Sons of Zadok" are mentioned in both the Zadokite Document and in the Manual of Discipline. In the Zadokite Document, the sons of Zadok are the legitimate priests as had been designated by the prophet Ezekiel (44:15). The following is taken from this Document: "...God has assured them by the hand of the prophet Ezekiel: 'The priests and the Levites and the sons of Zadok who kept the charge of my sanctuary while the children of Israel went astray from me shall come near me to serve me and shall stand before me to offer me fat and blood.' The priests are the converts of Israel who went out from the land of Judah; and the Levites are those who joined them. And the sons of Zadok are the chosen of Israel, the men named with a name who shall stand at the end of days."[7] In the other Qumran scroll, the Manual of Discipline, the sons of Zadok are mentioned as the priests of the Qumran community of Essenes. The name "Sons of Zadok" also might have been extended to all the members of the community since they were the Elect, or Chosen, of Israel. But it is obvious that the Sadducees, through the Zadokite priesthood, had much in common with the Essenes.

Whatever made these Israelites split into different sects is difficult to say. But it is interesting that the Sadducees are the only sect of the three not labeled by a possibly derogatory epithet. Does this mean that the Sadducees, themselves named

for the Zadokite priesthood, might have been responsible for the name "Pharisees," the "Separators,"
thereby suggesting that the Pharisees by their actions
or beliefs, had "separated" themselves from the main
body of Judaism? Does it mean, too, that the Sadducees, noting what they considered similarities between
another Jewish group and pagan priests of Artemis
called "Essenes," had applied this same name to the
Jewish group?

But regardless of who was responsible for be-
stowing the title on the Jewish group, the fact remains
that the name for the priests of Artemis and for
the Jewish community was the same:"Essenes," and
it may be safely assumed that the detractors of the
Jewish sect took full advantage of any similarities
which they thought they perceived between the two
groups, as will be seen.

That the Jewish Essenes were subject to ridicule
may be inferred from what the late Yigael Yadin stated
in an article in the September-October 1984 issue
of the Biblical Archaeology Review, in which the
noted archaeologist records some comments and con-
clusions concerning the Temple Scroll, the most recently discovered of the Dead Sea Scrolls and one
recently translated by Yadin. It was Yadin's theory
that the Essenes regarded Jerusalem in the same way
that they regarded the camp where the tabernacle
was kept during the wilderness period, and thus the
laws and prohibitions applicable to the wilderness
camp were equally applicable to the entire city of
Jerusalem. These laws, states Yadin, were applied
much more strictly by the Essenes than by normative
Judaism. The results in at least one situation were,
as Yadin puts it, quite "bizarre."

At one place in his Jewish War, Josephus makes
reference to the "gate of the Essenes" in Jerusalem,
a gate which has never been unearthed nor identified,
but has been equated with another gate mentioned
much earlier in history,the Dung Gate. Interestingly
enough, when Josephus mentions the Essene Gate, he
located it near a place called Bethso (V.147), which
Yadin points out is Beth-Soah in Hebrew, meaning
"lavatory.". There is every reason, too, to assume
that the Dung Gate, also never unearthed, had been
appropriately named, although modern expositors have
attempted to soften the impact on readers by maintaining that the Dung Gate was one through which
refuse in general or ashes were taken to be disposed

of. Euphemisms. however, are misleading. While the Hebrew term <u>ashpoth</u> may at times convey these meanings, the common meaning is "dung," "excrement," both human and animal. The gate apparently was one associated with dung or with people going to stool. In the absence of euphemisms, what then is the explanation?

The law referred to by Yadin as having bizarre results is found in Deuteronomy 23:12-14, which required a place outside the camp for defecation, the reason being that "the Lord your God walks in the midst of your camp...therefore your camp must be holy that he may not see anything indecent among you." Thus in the application of this law to the whole city of Jerusalem, the faithful would have to go outside the city to relieve themselves, a requirement which posed no special problem except on the seventh day. A command in Exodus 16:29 given by the Lord to Moses is "let no man go out of his place on the seventh day," which, if interpreted literally, would prohibit all pious Jews from defecating on that day since they would not be permitted to leave the city. But in the course of time this law came to be interpreted to mean that nobody should travel farther than 2000 cubits from his "place," Jerusalem. In fact the <u>War Scroll</u> of the Essenes has 2000 cubits as the allowable distance. It would seem, then, that with this interpretation the problem of defecation on the seventh day was solved. A person could obey the command to relieve himself outside the "camp," Jerusalem, and still technically remain there as long as he did not stray more than 2000 cubits.

But this was not enough for the ultra-pious Essenes. As Yadin states, the Temple Scroll not only forbids the building of toilets inside the city but forbids them within 3000 cubits of the city. This would place toilets beyond the allowable 2000 cubits, and thus the Essenes would not be able to relieve themselves on the seventh day. A possible reason for setting a distance of 3000 cubits is that according to the Temple Scroll, a toilet at 3000 cubits would not be visible from the city, implying that one would be visible at 2000 cubits. As indicated, the Law required that the Lord be spared from such offensive sights and Jerusalem was where He dwelt. By requiring toilets to be 3000 cubits from the city, the Essenes were imposing a real hardship on themselves.

21

Josephus confirms that the Essenes did not go to stool on the seventh day and explains that they were careful even on the other days of the week not to subject the Lord to the offensive sight. He states that the Essenes went to "remote spots" where they dug a slit trench with their mattocks, a spade-like tool furnished to all neophytes of the Order. They then wrapped their mantle about them so that they "may not offend the rays of the deity."[8] Afterward they replaced the excavated soil with their spade.

Thus by applying this part of the Law so strictly, the Essenes undoubtedly must have made themselves stand out conspicuously from the other citizens who did not apply the Law that strictly. At the end of the seventh day, the Essenes must have presented a laughable sight in their white robes and carrying their mattocks as they hurried toward the gate which until that time had been called Dung, but which was now colloquially named Essene Gate in derision of the Essenes, who, at the specified time each week, made a determined exit through it. Thus there seem to be ample grounds for the Essenes to be ridiculed, and it would not be unreasonable to assume that the name "Essene" itself was one of mockery.

But let us return to a consideration of the antiquity of the Essenes. If this sect went far back into history as claimed by all three, Pliny, Philo, and Josephus, the obvious question is why, then, were they never mentioned in ancient literature? The Jewish Encyclopedia attempts an answer by stating that the claim to antiquity stems from there being "types" of Essenes, named for well-known historical figures. One must confess that this explanation seems to lack clarity, and thus reasonable speculation must be relied upon for at least a temporary answer.

It is unfortunate that speculation is regarded so sceptically by scientists and critics of various kinds. It should not be forgotten that reasonable speculation is an important part of discovery and scientific achievement. Every true scientist has been guilty of speculation, from the early Greeks to Galileo to Einstein. It may also be remembered that the existence of the city of Troy rested upon mere speculation until its discovery by that dreamer, Heinrich Schliemann. It can be said that often it is speculation which directs archaeologists where to work. With this apology, let us proceed with what is hoped is reasonable speculation concerning the relatives and forebears of the Essenes.

The reference already cited in Philo's <u>Hypothetica</u> to the Essenes as disciples of Moses may contain the clue necessary to identify the ancestors of the Essenes. Philo, in that passage, noted that the "persuasion" or "vocation" of that group "is not based on birth, for birth is not a descriptive mark of voluntary associations, but on their <u>zeal</u> (italics mine) for virtue and desire to promote brotherly love."[9] Thus the "family tree" of the Essenes might be examined through the principle of "zeal," or what W. R. Farmer calls the "theology of zeal."[10] This theology of zeal can be traced back to Moses, and in so doing, we may be tracing and identifying the ancestors of the Essenes.

The terms <u>zeal</u> and <u>jealousy</u> have the same root in Hebrew, and the difference in meaning between the two is very slight. The theology of zeal can thus be traced back to the exodus and the Decalogue (Ten Commandments): "You shall not make yourself a graven image, or any likeness of anything that is in heaven above or that is in the earth beneath, or that is in the water under the earth; you shall not bow down to them or serve them; for I the Lord your God am a <u>jealous</u> God...." (Ex. 20:4-5) The Hebrew word for <u>jealous</u> in this passage is <u>qanna</u>, while the word for <u>zealous</u>, for example in Numbers 25:11, is <u>qana</u>. Likewise in the Septuagint, the ancient Greek translation of the Old Testament, the word used for <u>jealous</u> in the same Exodus passage is <u>zelotes</u>, which again, is the same word for <u>zeal</u>.

One may remember the story of Moses coming down from Mount Sinai, where he had received the Decalogue, and saw the Israelites indulging in worship of the golden calf. The "golden calf" was actually a young bull, and bull worship had been practiced by neighboting peoples for hundreds of years. The Hebrews were thus placing the worship of a "graven image" before the worship of Yahweh, their God. This so excited the wrath of Moses that he smashed the tablets and called upon all those on the "Lord's side" to slay all the apostate Israelites. We are told that the Levites responded, who then slew 3000 of their sinful brothers. As a reward for the faithful Levites, Moses stated that they had ordained themselves (Chapter 32 of Exodus), implying regular priesthood for their faithfulness and zeal in executing

23

the wrath of Yahweh. After this it can be noticed that the "men of zeal" were almost invariably priests or of priestly families.

It is interesting that Yahweh, when he renewed the covenant with Moses, repeated the commandment -but with a variation: "For you shall worship no other god, for the Lord, whose name is Jealous, is a jealous god." (Ex. 34:14) Again the Hebrew word is qanna, and zelotes in the Greek Septuagint. It would seem, then, that when the Israelites excited Yahweh's jealousy by apostasy, the propitiatory act performed by the men of zeal was in a sense prophylactic. Farmer compares them to a surgeon excising a cancerous tissue by extirpating the apostates of Israel with the sharp edge of the sword.[11] Then somewhere along the path of history, zeal for the God of the Covenant was transferred to his Law, and when this happened, the men of zeal felt impelled to kill not only any Jewish apostate, including themselves if the occasion demanded, but any non-Jew who had transgressed the Law.

Farmer lists from the Old Testament Simeon, Levi, Phinehas, and Elijah as being the exemplars par excellence of the men of zeal, and notes the priestly tradition carried on by each.[12] For present purposes, remarks can be limited to one: Phinehas. The story is told in Numbers 25. It seems that the Israelites were "playing the harlot" with alien women and worshipping their gods. The crisis came when an Israelite brought a Midianite woman into camp in view of everyone including Moses. Phinehas, noting the incident along with the others, took a spear and followed the man and woman into the "inner room," where he pierced both. The passage which follows is the one that Farmer claims to be the most important for understanding the theology of zeal: "And the Lord said to Moses, 'Phinehas the son of Eleazar, son of Aaron the priest, has turned back my wrath from the people of Israel, in that he was jealous with my jealousy among them, so that I did not consume the people of Israel in my jealousy. Therefore say, Behold, I give to him my covenant of peace; and it shall be to him, and to his descendants after him, the covenant of a perpetual priesthood, because he was jealous for his God, and made atonement for the people of Israel.'" (Numbers 25:10-13).

Thus if zeal were part of their theology, the

24

Essenes can be traced back to Moses, and they probably regarded themselves as a part of the "perpetual priesthood." But Philo, who also made the claim that the Essenes could be traced back to Moses, was misled when he stated that the zeal of the Essenes was for virtue and to promote brotherly love, although a man of zeal might be able to rationalize it to that extent. Zeal was composed of fanaticism and cruelty, although the claim was made that it was propitiatory and atoned for sin. The Jewish Encyclopedia puts it euphemistiacally when it maintains that the word came from zeal for the Law.

It was during the intertestamental period, the time-lapse between the Old Testament writings and those of the New Testament, that the theology of zeal was most strikingly evident in practice. Some of the writing that bridges these years is contained in the Apocrypha, meaning "Hidden Writings." These were Jewish documents which were believed by some should have been included in the official canon, and the dispute raised by this issue covered many years. Some of the books were included in the Septuagint, the Greek translation which was already in use by the time of Jesus. While the Protestant position has been that the books of the Apocrypha were not inspired, the Roman Catholic Church, since the Council of Trent in 1546, and the Greek Orthodox Church, since the Synod of Constantinople in 1638, have declared certain of these books to be inspired and thus have included them in their official canon.

Attention will be focused primarily on the First Book of the Maccabees. It relates the story of the Maccabean rebellion, an event which led not only to Jewish independence for a time, but also to the establishment of the priest-king dynasty of the Hasmoneans.

First, however, a bit of background might be useful to those not familiar with the period. It will be remembered that Alexander the Great conquered Palestine in 333 BC. but died in Babylon ten years later from overindulgence in alcohol and general debauchery. Following Alexander's death, Palestine came under the control of the dynasty founded in Egypt by one of Alexander's generals, Ptolemy, and remained so until 198 BC. After that date, it came under control of the dynasty established in Syria by another general, Seleucus. Under the Seleucid kings, the Jews underwent much suffering and outrage, until they revolted under the so-called Maccabees in 167 BC.

The events which were the immediate cause of the rebellion are worth relating. The Seleucid monarch at the time was Antiochus IV, who called himself "Epiphanes," literally meaning "Appearance" but in reality meaning "Appearance of God," an epithet which hardly endured him to the Jews. He attempted to suppress the Jewish religion, for he believed that all peoples should be one in religion, law, and custom. While some Jews did submit, one group refused. Antiochus then ordered sterner measures and instituted specific regulations against the sabbath, circumcision, and possessing the Book of the Law. The penalty for breaking these regulations was death. But there was still resistance. Then the ultimate occurred when an altar to Zeus was erected over the altar of burnt offering in the Temple. Many Jews, of course, could not tolerate such an abomination, and when violence flared, many were put to death.

The time was ripe for open rebellion, and the match which set the conflagration was lit in the village of Modin near Jerusalem. Present in the village at the time were the male members of a priestly family named Hasmon. At the head was Mattathias, and with him his five sons, John, Simon, Judas, Eleazar, and Jonathan. These Hasmoneans also became known as the "Maccabees," or the "Hammers," especially Judas because of his military feats against the Syrians during the rebellion. I Maccabees relates the story (trans. New English Bible):

"The king's officers who were forcing apostasy came to the town of Modin to see that sacrifice was offered, and many Israelites went over to them. Mattathias and his sons stood in a group. The king's officers spoke to Mattathias: 'You are a leader here,' they said, 'a man of mark and influence in this town, with your sons and brothers at your back. You be the first now to come forward and carry out the king's order. All the nations have done so, as well as the leading men in Judaea and the people left in Jerusalem. Then you and your sons will be enrolled among the King's Friends; you will all receive high honours, rich rewards of silver and gold, and many further benefits.'

"To this Mattathias replied in a ringing voice: 'Though all the nations within the king's dominions

26

obey him and forget their ancestral worship, though they have chosen to submit to his commands, yet I and my sons and brothers will follow the covenant of our fathers. Heaven forbid we should ever abandon the law and its statutes. We will not obey the command of the king, nor will we deviate one step from our forms of worship.'

"As soon as he had finished, a Jew stepped forward in full view of all to offer sacrifice on the pagan altar at Modin, in obedience to the royal command. The sight stirred Mattathias to indignation; he shook with passion, and in a fury of righteous anger, rushed forward and slaughtered the traitor on the very altar. At the same time he killed the officer sent by the king to enforce sacrifice, and pulled the pagan altar down. Thus <u>Mattathias showed his fervent zeal for the law, just as Phinehas had done</u> by killing Zimri son of Salu. 'Follow me, he shouted through the town, '<u>every one of you who is zealous for the law and strives to maintain the covenant.</u>' (italics mine) He and his sons took to the hills, leaving all their belongings behind in the town."[13]

A number of items in the story are noteworthy. First, as was indicated, the Hasmonean family was the most influential and important, at least partially because of their priestly status, a status which followed the tradition of zeal. This was the reason the king's officer made an attempt to enlist the help of Mattathias and his sons - an old military trick which this time did not work.

Second, in his "fervent zeal for the law," Mattathias slaughtered both the traitorous Jew and the king's officer, both Jew and non-Jew, as Phinehas had done earlier, and who is even referred to by Mattathias as a great exemplar. It is again noteworthy that on his deathbed, Mattathias once more paid tribute to Phinehas as "our father" who "never flagged in his zeal and his was a covenant of an everlasting priesthood."[14] There is no question that Mattathias followed the theology of zeal begun at the time of Moses.

Third, it is maintained by some that when Mattathias made his move at Modin with his rallying cry, the group known as the Zealots was born. Although the terms <u>zeal</u> and <u>zealous</u> are used in the Old Testa-

27

ment, <u>zealot</u> is not used, either to denote a member of a group or otherwise. Accordingly, up to this point we have avoided the use of the word <u>Zealot</u> and have used in its place "men of zeal." Yet we know from the writing of Josephus and others that a group called "Zealots" was active during the Roman period until the fall of Masada in 73 AD. and possibly until the second rebellion against Rome under Bar Kokhba in the second century AD. It is possible, therefore, that a group called Zealots might have had its origin with the Maccabees. Nevertheless, it should be kept firmly in mind that the theology of zeal was followed throughout the Old Testament by outstanding Israelites, and that Mattathias and his sons carried on this "theology."

The rebellion itself achieved a great deal of success especially under the son Judas, following the death of Mattathias, a success due at least in part to a militant sect called the Hasideans, who had joined forces with the Maccabees. These Hasideans are thought by some scholars to have been the precursors of the Essenes.[15] Their name is usually translated "Saints," or at times "Faithful Ones." They are mentioned in a few psalms, including 149, part of which is reproduced here because of what it reveals about the group:

> Sing to the Lord a new song,
> sing his praise in the assembly of
> the faithful (Hasideans)
> ...
> Let his faithful servants (Hasideans)
>   exult in triumph;
> let them shout for joy as they kneel
>   before him.
> Let the high praises of God be on their
>   lips and a two-edged sword in
>   their hand,
> To wreak vengeance on the nations
>   and to chastise the heathen;
> to load their kings with chains
>   and to put their nobles in irons;
> to execute the judgment decreed against
>   them -
> this is the glory of all his faithful
>   servants (Hasideans)

New English Bible

Thus is pictured in this psalm an organization of ones faithful to the Lord, trusting in Him, and specially chosen to zealously attack His enemies.

During the Maccabean rebellion, the Hasideans lived up to the praise of the psalmist. I Maccabees relates how the Maccabees were joined by a company of Hasideans, "stalwarts of Israel, everyone of them a volunteer in the cause of the law."(2:42) It is of interest that "volunteers" was one of the terms used by the writers of the Scrolls to refer to them-selves - the Essenes. Then in a passage in II Mac-cabees (14:1-6) it is related how a treacherous Jew by the name of Alcimus, who formerly had been a high priest, had been summoned by the Seleucid ruler to be questioned about the attitude and the plans of the Jews. Alcimus replied, "Those of the Jews who are called Hasideans and are led by Judas Maccabeus are keeping the war alive and fomenting sedition, refusing to leave the country in peace." But unfor-tunately when the victorious Maccabees went on from their achievement of gaining religious liberty to the struggle for political independence and power, the Hasideans split with the Maccabees. It was then that the same treacherous Jew, Alcimus, slew a great number of the Hasideans, and they seemed from that time to have disappeared from the scene - at least under that name. But the possibility remains that a sect such as the Essenes may have continued every-thing but the name.

Many scholars, including Oesterreicher, Rowley, Howlett, and Burrows, believe that the origin of the Essenes did indeed lie with the Hasideans. More-over, the Jewish Encyclopedia claims that even the Essenes admitted this relationship. Thus it may well be that the Hasideans were precursors of the Essenes. But if such was the case, so must have been the Hasmoneans, around whom the Hasideans had rallied - that is, if the theology of zeal is used as the common denominator. For the rebellion was under the leadership of the Hasmoneans, and, as noted above, Alcimus in his report stated that the Hasideans were led by Judas Maccabeus.

There will undoubtedly be criticism of the idea that the Hasmoneans were precursors of the Essenes, especially when one considers the relations existing between the Essenes and those Hasmonean rulers who held the throne at the time the Essenes actually existed by that name. However, it should be repeated that the forebears of the Essenes are being traced through the theology of zeal, and Mattathias and his sons have to be the outstanding examples of men of zeal at that time in Jewish history. In fact, W. R. Farmer stresses the importance of the Hasmoneans, or Maccabees, in the line of men of zeal.[16]

A few words concerning the Hasmonean dynasty might prove helpful. With the successful conclusion of the Maccabean Rebellion, the reign of the Hasmoneans began and it lasted until Herod the Great came to the throne in 37 BC. During the rebellion, after Judas had died in battle, his brother Jonathan became the military leader and finally gained independence from Syrian sovereignty. Jonathan was smart enough to have himself appointed by the Seleucid monarch to the office of high priest, the office carrying the ruling powers with it. The office also became hereditary from that time on.

Jonathan, upon his death, was succeeded by his brother Simon, who was granted by his own people the title of "ethnarch," or governor, and the right of succession was also granted to his heirs. Of course he had already succeeded to the high priesthood with the death of Jonathan. Thus the Hasmonean dynasty was firmly established. Simon is often considered the best ruler the Jews had during the post-exilic period, but his rule lasted only six years - from 141 to 135 BC.

The son who succeeded Simon was John Hyrcanus, who greatly increased his prestige during his rule (135-105 BC.). His sympathies seemed to have leaned toward the Hellenistically-inclined group, as we can note the Greek names given to the Hasmoneans thereafter. Two matters concerning Hyrcanus are worthy of note. First, it may be that he was the first of the Hasmoneans to assume the title of king, although most scholars believe that his son, Judas Aristobulus I, was the daring one. Be that as it may, all the previous Hasmoneans had ruled in every way except having the title of king. But from this time on, they ruled both as king and as high priest - that is, with the exception of Alexandra, whom we shall meet in a moment. The second matter in the reign of John Hyrcanus that is worthy of consideration is that coins from his regime have been found at the site of the Essene settlement at Qumran, impressive evidence that the sect had by that time come into existence by that name.

Other priest kings followed, but by this time the character of the rulers, with the acquisition of power, had changed drastically. Alexander Jannaeus, according to Josephus, was guilty of atrocities incredible in their savagery.[17] Jannaeus, ruling from 104 to 78 BC., is considered by some to be the "Wicked Priest,", who, in the Scroll of the Commentary on Habakkuk, persecuted the Teacher of Righteousness (or Correct Expositor, as Theodor Gaster prefers). Jannaeus has also been identified as the Lion of Wrath in the Nahum Commentary. He undoubtedly was one of the most unsavory characters in Jewish history.

Then there appeared in the line of Hasmonean rulers a queen - Alexandra, or Salome to give her her Hebrew name. We are told that she ruled wisely and well during her nine-year reign, although of course the high priesthood had to be invested in her older son, Hyrcanus II, who also has been identified as the Wicked Priest because of his behavior during his reign. For present purposes, the matter of note is that the nature of each of Alexandra's two sons was such that an Idumean named Antipater was able to begin a cabal which ultimately resulted in the beheading of Antigonus, the last of the Hasmonean kings, in 37 BC. and the usurpation of the throne by Antipater's son Herod, called the Great.

One must say that the Hasmonean rule had degenerated shamefully from the days of Judas and Jonathan. Mattathias and his sons were certainly men of zeal, as were those who allied themselves with the rebellion, such as the Hasideans. But as the power of the Hasmoneans increased, so did their corruption and cruelty. Former allies dissociated themselves from the rulers, bringing about persecution by the priest-kings. Two became known to the Essenes as the Wicked Priest, as already noted, and the Man of the Lie. Dupont-Sommer claims that this historical era is reflected in a section of the Testament of Levi, fragments of which were found at Qumran. It is so important for the understanding of the Hasmonean period that it is reproduced here:

"And as you have heard tell concerning
    the seventy years,
hear tell also concerning the priesthood.
For to every jubilee shall correspond a
    priesthood.

And during the first jubilee, the first

31

Anointed to the priesthood shall be
  great;
and he shall speak to God as to a father,
and his priesthood shall be fully with
  the Lord,
and in his joyful days he shall arise for
  the salvation of the world.

In the second jubilee, the Anointed shall
  be promoted because of the mourning
  of a loved one,
and his priesthood shall be honoured
and he shall be glorified by all.

As for the third priest, he shall vanish
  sadly.

And the fourth shall be in sorrows,
for iniquity shall be heaped upon him in
  abundance
and all (the children of) Israel shall
  hate one another.

The fifth shall vanish into darkness:
likewise also the sixth and seventh.

Now in the seventh (jubilee), there shall
  be a defilement
(such) that I cannot speak of (it) before
  men;
for they shall know it who shall commit
  it!
Because of this they shall be taken captive
  and shall be plundered,
and their land and possessions shall be
  destroyed..."[18]

Dupont-Sommer claims that this apocalypse en-
visages historical reality - seven priests, succeeding
one another as in a dynasty, one which began so
gloriously but ended in misery and crime.[19]

The early Hasmoneans were indeed men of zeal,
as were the Hasideans. The zeal of the Essenes,
perhaps the descendants of the Hasideans, will be
discussed in the following chapter. But one matter
must be emphasized: the ancestral line of zeal is
not being traced by mere physical or psychological
similarity such as great courage or a fanatic sense
of nationalism. Their zeal was founded in their

strict adherence to the Mosaic Law, particularly to what some call the Second Commandment or the Second Word. Any deviation from this Second Commandment by any person or group of persons would be met with the utmost violence by Men of Zeal. They were the watch-dogs for a Jealous God.

NOTES TO CHAPTER II

1. Josephus, _Antiquities_, XVIII.11.

2. Pliny, V.73.

3. Philo, _Hypothetica_, 7.19-11.

4. A. Powell Davies, _The Meaning of the Dead Sea Scrolls_ (New York: New American Library, 1956), p. 61-62.

5. _Ibid._

6. W. R. Farmer, "Essenes," _The Interpreter's Dictionary of the Bible_ (New York: Abingdon Press, 1962).

7. Dupont-Sommer, p. 126-127.

8. Josephus, _War_ II. 148-149.

9. Philo, _Hypothetica_ 7.19-11.

10. Farmer, "Essenes," _Interpreter's Dictionary of the Bible_.

11. _Ibid._, "Zealot."

12. _Ibid._

13. I Maccabees 2:15-28.

14. _Ibid._, 2:54

15. See Duncan Howlett, _The Essenes and Christianity_.

16. W. R. Farmer, _Maccabees, Zealots, and Josephus_ (New York: Columbia, 1956), Chapter V.

17. Josephus, _War_, I.97.

18. Dupont-Sommer, p. 354.

19. _Ibid._

CHAPTER III

ZEALOTS, SICARII, AND ESSENES

In the last chapter one matter concerning Jonathan, brother of Judas Maccabeus was not mentioned: he saw the practical use of a mesa atop a great rock on the southwest shore of the Dead Sea, a rock which rises precipitously for 1300 feet above the shore. The top has the shape of a diamond with an area of about eighteen acres, which is accessible from only two sides, but not without great difficulty. Josephus describes the rock, and his description is indeed accurate: "A rock of no slight circumference and lofty from end to end is abruptly terminated on every side by deep ravines, the precipices rising sheer from an invisible base and being inaccessible to the foot of any living creature, save in two places where the rock permits of no easy ascent. Of these tracks one leads from the Lake Asphaltitis (Dead Sea) on the east, the other by which the approach is easier, from the west. The former they call the snake, seeing a resemblance to that reptile in its narrowness and continual windings; for its course is broken in skirting the jutting crags and, returning frequently upon itself and gradually lengthening out again, it makes painful headway. One traversing this route must firmly plant each foot alternately. Destruction faces him; for on either side yawn chasms so terrific as to daunt the hardiest. After following this perilous track for thirty furlongs, one reaches the summit, which, instead of tapering to a sharp peak, expands into a plain."

Jonathan realized the possibilities this great rock had for defense and erected a fortress on the mesa, calling it Masada, meaning "Fortress." Later, King Herod added to the defenses for his own protection against the Jews. Following Herod's death, it was garrisoned by the Romans until the start of the Jewish war against Rome in 66 AD. when it was captured by the Jews. After that, the story of Masada becomes an epic one, which covers the next seven years. Excavations were made at Masada from 1963 to 1965 by the distinguished soldier-archaeologist, the late Yigael Yadin, who found Josephus's account to be remarkably exact. This great fortress will be referred to often during this chapter.

From the latter days of the Hasmoneans through

35

through the reigns of Herod and his successors, right to the time of the war between the Jews and Rome, the situation in Judea was indeed chaotic. The plots, counterplots, machinations, intrigues, schemes, assassinations and killings are hard to exaggerate. The Romans could not understand people who seemed to them to be religious fanatics, while the Jews could not tolerate sacrilege. The Roman emperor, Caligula, ordered his statue to be set up in the Temple but rescinded the order at the request of Herod Agrippa, who, history tells us, was the last king of the Jews, dying in 44 AD. Caligula would have probably reissued the order if he had not been assassinated. After that, all Palestine was under Roman rule.

Judean affairs went from bad to worse, both between the Romans and Jews and among the Jews themselves. Brigandage was commonplace. Nobody remained long in jail who could afford a bribe to pay for his release. There was no responsible government. Gessius Florus, the nominal leader from 64 to 66 AD., was responsible for murder and massacre, and at last was driven by the populace from Jerusalem, where the Jews murdered the Roman garrison, even after the garrison had surrendered. This, of course, was rebellion and a signal for war.

To better understand this period of violence, one must return to the Jewish sects and the men of zeal. If we pick up the trail of those who followed the theology of zeal from the time of Herod the Great in 37 BC. to the fall of Masada in 73 AD., we are led straight to the Zealots. When the name Zealot was first applied is not known for certain, possibly as some believe about 6 BC., or as others believe, when Mattathias first sounded the call for men of zeal in 167 BC. But whenever it occurred, there is no doubt that the Zealots earned the name. They were the Jewish nationalists during the century before the Jewish war with Rome. Josephus in his Antiquities describes a "fourth philosophy," and while he nowhere mentions the name of the sect, scholars have generally assumed that he was describing the Zealots, crediting their founding to a certain Judas the Galileean:

"As for the fourth of the philosophies, Judas the Galileean set himself up as leader of it. This school agrees in all other respects with the opinions of the Pharisees, except that they have a passion for liberty that is almost unconquerable, since they are convinced that God alone is their leader and master. They think little of submitting to death in unusual forms and permitting vengeance to fall on kinsmen and friends if only they may avoid calling any man master. Inasmuch as most people have seen the steadfastness of their resolution amid such circumstances, I may forego any other account. For I have no fear that anything reported of them will be considered incredible. The danger is, rather, that report may minimize the indifference with which they accept the grinding misery of pain. The folly that ensued began to afflict the nation after Gessius Florus, who was governor, had by his overbearing and lawless actions provoked a desperate rebellion against the Romans...."[2]

Earlier, Josephus had claimed only three "philosophies" for the Jews: the Sadducees, Pharisees, and Essenes. Why he should add this fourth later on is not clear. Perhaps he was attempting to dissociate the Essenes from the Zealots. He admired the Essenes greatly, but in his view the Zealots were criminals of the worst sort, and he even objected to the name "Zealots" being used for the group, referring to them as "so-called Zealots."[3] In another passage he angrily stated that "...these miscreants called themselves (Zealots) as though they were zealous in the cause of virtue and not for vice in its basest and most extravagant form."[4] An important consideration here is that it is obvious from what Josephus has written that the word <u>Zealot</u> itself is not objectionable; it only became so when it was used by some who, in the eyes of Josephus, were prostituting the original concept of being zealous for the Lord or for the Law. Josephus had apparently forgotten how the Levites at the time of the exodus had slain thousands of brother Jews for their apostasy, and how Phinehas had killed the Hebrew and the Midianite woman. The Zealots were following the strict tradition of the theology of zeal.

During the Hasmonean years, the men of zeal had been relatively quiet. The early Hasmoneans had, of course, been men of zeal themselves, but even with the degeneration of the dynasty and the cruelty of rulers like the Wicked Priest, there was still quiet, possibly because of the oath taken by the Essenes to support their rulers. But when Herod, an Idumean, usurped the throne, men of zeal began to stir restlessly. Then Herod committed some atrocious murders to assure the end of the Hasmonean

37

and therefore her two sons by Herod, Alexander and Aristobulus, also were Hasmoneans and as such were eligible to assume the throne. Thus to make sure that there would be no restoration of the Hasmonean line, Herod would have to murder his own wife and two sons. Which he did.

The Zealots (as we shall now call them instead of "men of zeal") then became active, their purpose apparently to punish the crimes of bloodshed, as well as idolatry, committed by Herod. But as the years passed and Roman tyranny increased, the Zealots turned most of their activity against the Romans and Roman sympathizers. Then Zealots appeared in Jerusalem with daggers hidden beneath their cloaks, and in time they became incredibly adept at using the daggers and also being able to escape all retaliation. In fact, they became so clever at assassination that they became known as <u>sicarii</u>, a Latin word meaning "stabbers." Since <u>sicarii</u>(singular <u>sicarius</u>) is Latin, it is safe to assume that it was a term used by the Romans for the Zealots, who waged a guerilla-type warfare against them. But the Romans were not the only victims of the sicarii. Those Jews who tried to make some sort of accomodation with the Romans, or even some who remained neutral, became victims of the daggers. Josephus thought of these killers as the worst of Jewish criminals, who not only killed their own people, he maintained, but also destroyed their property. The historian adds that the sicarii regarded such Jews who collaborated with the Romans as no others but aliens who "ignobly sacrificed the hard-won liberty of the Jews and admitted their preference for the Roman yoke."[5] This picture represents the viewpoint of many scholars, that the sicarii were the more extreme segment of the Zealots.

But it has been more than hinted here that the Zealots also had some sort of relationship with the Essenes. What was that relationship? For an answer, we can appeal to Hippolytus and the <u>Jewish Encyclopedia</u>. Hippolytus, the Church father mentioned earlier as one of our sources for our knowledge of the Essenes, was much disturbed about the different Jewish factions, for as he saw it, every sect was founded upon some heresy, a heresy based upon a departure from the word of God as revealed to Moses. These heresies, of course, had to be refuted by Hippolytus, and he stated that to do so, he intended to examine the three main sects, the Pharisees, Sadducees,and Essenes.

Hippolytus writes as if he considered the Essenes to be the foremost of the three, devoting to them nine-and-a-half chapters, as compared to one chapter to the Sadducees, and one-half chapter to the Pharisees.[6] The chapter that includes the Pharisees is ambiguous enough for one to gain the impression that they were a division of the Essenes[7] - which they might have been.

Hippolytus further claimed that the Essenes were comprised of four "parties," some disciplining themselves more than the rules of the Order required. Some would not even handle a coin, maintaining that they ought not to carry, behold, or fashion an image. Others would not go through a gate into a city lest they walk under a statue, i.e. an image of some sort. Still others would not touch the younger members of the Order, or if they happened to do so by accident, they immediately resorted to ablution to cleanse themselves.[8] The Essenes must have given Hippolytus all sorts of difficulty in refuting so many heresies.

Then Hippolytus gives a most significant item of information, information which departs drastically from any given by Josephus or Philo. He maintains that if the members of one party of Essenes hears a person discussing God or the Law, and if they believe this person to be uncircumcised, they will threaten him with death (at an opportune moment when he was alone) if he refuses to undergo the rite of circumcision. If the person does not wish to comply with this "request," the Essenes slaughter him. From such activities, states Hippolytus, the Essenes had gained the name Zealots from some, and from others, Sicarii.[9] In other words, Hippolytus believed not only that the Essenes were men of zeal, but that the Zealots and Sicarii were "parties" of Essenes. Such a claim is either ignored or resisted by many scholars, yet the Jewish Encyclopedia supports this statement, clearly asserting that the Zealots and Sicarii were Essenes (under "Essene"). It will be shown that this theory answers a number of puzzling questions.

Having submitted evidence of the likelihood that the Zealots and Sicarii were parties of Essenes, let us now return to the war with Rome. To meet this crisis, the Jews set up an emergency government with the Pharisees in control. Josephus, a Pharisee, who happily for posterity, became better known as an historian than as a soldier, was placed in charge in charge of the defense of Galilee. He apparently fought bravely, but was defeated and then defected to the Romans. The nationalistic element of the Jews, the Zealot-Sicarii-Essenes, believed Josephus had fought only half-heartedly and then had become a traitor, and consequently they took over the reins from the Pharisees. All moderation was at an end.

If Israel had been united, the war might have gone differently. As it was, Israel did have its moments, thanks largely to the Zealots-Essenes. Masada, the fortress referred to earlier, had been in the hands of the Romans during the period of the provincial governors in Judea-6 to 66 AD. - but was captured from them by Menahem, the son of Judas the Galileean, the one given credit by Josephus for founding the Zealots as a political party. In the hands of the Zealots, the fortress then remained a focal point for their activity throughout the war.[10] Josephus also relates[11] how a whole Roman army under Cestius was annihilated by the Jews during this campaign. According to the Jewish Encyclopedia, this tremendous victory was achieved mainly by the Zealots, and the year 66 AD. was prematurely celebrated as the year of deliverance from Rome.

But the Jews were not united, and Jerusalem was torn by factional strife. Jews massacred Jews, rivaling the slaughter by the Romans, and the war became a hopeless one for the Jews. In 70 AD. the outer court of the Temple was set afire, and fighting went on around the inner altar. The Temple fell just as Jesus had predicted "with not one stone upon another." (Matt. 24:02)

Jewish opposition, however, did not end with the capture of Jerusalem and the destruction of the Temple. The fortress of Masada, captured only a few years earlier by the Jews, held out until 73 or 74 AD. (there is disagreement as to which year) when the Roman forces under their most renowned general, Flavius Silva, managed to breach the walls by first erecting an enormous ramp on the west side of the rock. The story of how the last defenders held the Romans at bay for three years and preferred self-imposed death to capture by the Romans is a moving and a well-known one, a terrible and glorious page in the history of the Jewish people. When the capture of Masada was imminent, the defenders under the leadership of Eleazar ben Ya'ir planned how they would destroy themselves, and when the time arrived, the final man died believing himself to be the last of the defenders. However, there turned out to be seven survivors, two old women and five children. Even the Romans, we are told, admired the courage of this band.[12]

The identity of the Jewish defenders of Masada is well established, although there has been some confusion because of the tendency to separate the Zealots, Sicarii, and Essenes into separate compartments.[13] Josephus had referred to the defenders as Sicarii,[13] but Yigael Yadin uses the name "Zealots." In fact, the subtitle of his noted volume Masada is "Herod's Fortress and the Zealots' Last Stand." On one occasion, however, he refers to scholars who have called them "Sicarii Zealots."[14] This is a reflection of the viewpoint held by many scholars that the Sicarii were a branch of the Zealots.

But two Oxford scholars, Sir Godfrey Driver and Cecil Roth, while subscribing to the theory that the defenders of Masada were Zealots, carried this theory a step farther. In the late 50's they made the proposal that the people of the Qumran community also were Zealots,[15] and then postulated that since the Qumran sect and the defenders of Masada were all Zealots, there must have been a Republic of Masadah-Qumran.[16] Regardless of whether there ever was a "Republic," the important matter here is that two scholars perceived a connection between the Essenes of Qumran and those who defended Masada, although they did not refer to those at Qumran as Essenes but as Zealots.

Yadin does not agree that the Qumranites were Zealots. The evidence that they were indeed Essenes is too strong, he maintains. Yet Yadin himself is responsible for substantiating without doubt that a connection did exist between the Qumran group and those of Masada. In his excavations at Masada in 1963-65, he made a number of exciting discoveries of fragments of ancient scrolls. Altogether, portions of fourteen scrolls were discovered, biblical, sectarian, and apochryphal. Among the biblical scrolls were fragments of Psalms, Leviticus, Genesis, Ezekiel, and Deuteronomy. But the scroll which provided the biggest surprise was a sectarian one called "Songs of the Sabbath Sacrifices," for it was exactly the same as the text of a scroll discovered in Cave IV at Qumran.[17] To account for the scroll's presence at Masada, Yadin rejected Driver and Roth's theory that those of Qumran were Zealots. Rather, he states, the Essenes at Qumran were actually much more militant than has usually been thought and that they had taken a significant part in the rebellion and in the defense of Masada. It would be natural, then, he thought, for those at Masada to have brought with them their holy writing. He believes that Philo was mostly responsible for the image of the Essenes as pacifists and that Philo was in error on this point.[18]

Yadin, from this view, was undoubtedly correct in his claim of the militancy of the Essenes and their taking a significant part in the rebellion and in the defense of Masada, as well as being correct in his explanation of the presence of the scroll at Masada. But Driver and Roth could also be partially correct, although we do not subscribe to the "Republic" theory. It seems that this tendency to place groups in separate compartments is responsible for many disagreements. Would not the simplest explanation be that Hippolytus was right, that the Zealots, Sicarii, and Essenes were all one?

In assuming that the three sects were actually one, one recalls the heritage of the Essenes. They were at least the spiritual descendants of the Hasideans, the stalwarts of Israel who took their place alongside the Maccabees, and as has already been pointed out, the Essenes took pride in this relationship. Farmer points out, too, that there was a full conscious continuity of Jewish nationalism from the time of the Maccabees through the Roman period.[19] It is most difficult to understand this unless the assumption is made that both the Zealots and Sicarii were also Essenes.

The picture of the Essenes as peaceful ascetics leading a quiet monastic life by the Dead Sea is misleading to the point of being untrue. Josephus is more realistic. His contention that the Essenes bore arms for protection against brigands has already been cited. But also consider this passage describing the bravery of the Essenes in the face of death at the hands of the enemy: "They (the Essenes) make light of danger, and triumph over pain by their resolute will; death, if it come with honor, they consider better than immortality. The war with Rome tried their souls through and through by every variety of test. Racked and twisted, burnt and broken, and made to pass through every instrument of torture, in order to induce them to blaspheme their lawgiver

42

or to eat some forbidden thing, they refused to yield to either demand, nor ever once did they cringe to their persecutors or shed a tear. Smiling in their agonies and mildly deriding their tormentors, they cheerfully resigned their souls, confident that they would receive them back again..."[20] While a case could be made that Josephus was describing what the Romans did to some Essenes who would not defend themselves, the possibility seems highly unlikely, for these Essenes, it will be remembered, had been required to swear an oath that they would always fight for justice.

There is also internal evidence in the scrolls which points to the Essenes as a militant group well-versed in warfare. One of the scrolls is called "The War of the Sons of Light and the Sons of Darkness," or more simply "The War Scroll." It is almost impossible to read this without becoming convinced that the Essenes were indeed militant. Theodor Gaster, in speaking of this scroll, states that the Essenes regarded themselves as the militia of God, a kind of Salvation Army, ready like their ancestors under Moses and Joshua, as well as the Maccabees, to do battle for His name and to drive the heathen from His land - in this case, from the whole earth. Indeed, says Gaster, it sometimes called its adherents the "volunteers," a name with distinctly military overtones. There was even drawn up an elaborate plan for Armageddon, the final battle.[21] The plan, interestingly enough, showed a knowledge of Roman military tactics.

There is an important passage in the "War Scroll" which should be noted: "   and down on earth Thou hast (likewise) placed at thy service the elect of a holy people." The word "elect" is one of the terms by which the Essenes identified themselves. But in addition, Gaster points out in a footnote that it means " picked troops."[22]

Those who believe in the pacifism of the Essenes maintain that the "War Scroll" has to do' with the Last Days, the time of the final conflagration when the Messiah finally is to appear. This might be true, of course, but as calamity followed calamity, the Essenes might well have believed that the Day of God had at last arrived and that they were being called upon to fight the Sons of Darkness. The moon, it is true, had not yet "turned into blood," but destruction had come to the "evil ones" who had ruled

43

in Israel, and it was time now for God to turn his hand against the Kittim (the name used for the Romans).

Farmer has stated the situation well. He is convinced that a careful reading of the War Scroll makes it perfectly clear that with the Qumran community we are dealing with a group of Jewish patriots for whom there is absolutely no conflict between religion and patriotism, prayer and the sword. Their patriotism, he continues, grows out of their religion, their nationalism out of their piety, and the sword with which they strike is a consecrated weapon. The very strength with which they strike is a strength from God.[23]

And so Philo's image of the Essenes as pacifist ascetics fades. In its place there emerges into view a community whose heritage of nationalistic militancy, or zeal, goes far back into history, to the Exodus and the Decalogue. The Order required an oath of its initiates to do battle for the just, whose members faced the Roman war machine with steadfastness, and whose knowledge of Roman military tactics allowed them to defeat the Romans on important occasions. They even put their own countrymen to the sword if there was the slightest suspicion of apostasy, secure in their belief that they were upholding the Lord's Law. The theology of zeal, or "jealousy" for the Lord and His Law, was followed by these Jewish nationalists whether they were called Zealots, Sicarii, or Essenes, for they were united in that concept.

So with the fall of Masada came the end of the Zealots - Sicarii - Essenes. The end of the settlement at Qumran had come earlier. In 68 AD., those who had remained at Qumran, probably the scribes, saw the approach of the inevitable. They then took their precious manuscripts and climbed laboriously to the almost-inaccessible caves where the scrolls were deposited and where they remained hidden until the spring of 1947 when a Bedouin shepherd found them. The Romans, in all probability, had realized that some of the nationalists had come from the settlement and thus destroyed it, for what other reason could there be for destroying a monastery in the middle of the Judean wilderness? If there were any scribes or others remaining, the Romans wiped them out. It thus appears that during the course of the war, the Essenes of Qumran had been totally annihilated, for none ever returned to claim the hidden scrolls, leaving them for the shepherds to find almost two thousand years later.

As the years went by, the Essenes seemed to have dropped almost completely out of sight - and it was not by accident, for both Jews and Christians attempted to suppress even the name "Essene." Dupont-Sommer describes the attempt made by the Jewish community:

"After this great national catastrophe (the war with Rome), Israel reorganized itself in order to survive, and it was essentially the Rabbis - i.e. the Pharisees - who achieved this restoration and became the leaders of the New Synagogue. Deprived of its Temple, its ancient political machinery and of its land, it had to find the principle of unity and cohesion for the communities dispersed all over the world in the fervent love of its Book, the Torah, and in fidelity to the traditional interpretation of Scripture. In this New Synagogue, rebuilt and controlled by the Pharisees, and obliged, in order to resist more strongly, to harden itself within a unified discipline, the Essenes - who had previously been considered by Judaism as orthodox - found themselves cast aside, treated as undesirables, and after some time even hunted down as heretics and excommunicated. Inheriting these hostile sentiments, certain modern Jewish historians have been little inclined to show consideration for a sect which the official Synagogue formerly cursed and expelled."[24]

As far as the Christians are concerned, Dupont-Sommer points out that their historians, too, have not always done justice to the Essenes - but for different reasons. The Essenes, he states, present too many striking analogies to the primitive church, with the same beliefs, the same moral and mystical ideas and the same characteristic rites. A few brave souls, he continues, attempted to point out these analogies and even suggested that Christianity itself was a kind of Essenism. Such views by these Christian historians and theologians could hardly be tolerated and even the name became suspect.[25] Thus in 1947 when the Scrolls were discovered, what was a new word appeared to the layman: Essenes.

And so for many years the name of "Essenes" was practically obliterated, but the nationalistic side of Judaism was never entirely suppressed. During

the second century AD., another bloody uprising
against Rome took place, led by the warrior Simon
ben Kosiba, an able leader, whose name was changed
by Akiba, the foremost rabbi of the time, to Bar
Kokhba, "Son of the Star." Akiba also hailed Simon
as the Messiah, Bar Kokhba taking on the title "Prince
of Israel." The Jewish forces under Bar Kokhba had
startling success against the Romans for a time,
but greatly superior forces and the Roman tactics
gradually wore them down until Bar Kokhba himself
was killed at Bethar. The remnants of his army made
a stand in caves along the Dead Sea at Ein Gedi,
and like those at Masada held out to the last man,
preferring death to surrender. And so in 135 AD.
Judea was finished and its inhabitants scattered
widely over the then-known world.

It is most fitting that after eighteen centuries,
another soldier of Israel, Yigael Yadin, also regarded as one of the great archaeologists of the
country, should be the one to unearth the remains
left by the former fighters of Israel, at both Masada
and Ein Gedi. Israel had come back. And what a
striking coincidence that Jewish nationalism revived
at the same time the Essenic manuscripts from Qumran
were resurrected.

Caves at Qumran where first discoveries were made

NOTES TO CHAPTER III

1. Josephus, <u>War</u> VII. 280-284.

2. <u>Ibid.</u>, <u>Antiquities</u>. XVIII. 23.

3. <u>Ibid.</u>, <u>War</u> VII. 268.

4. <u>Ibid.</u>, <u>War</u> IV. 161.

5. <u>Ibid.</u> <u>War</u> VII.225.

6. Hippolytus, Book IX, Chapters XIII-XXIV.

7. <u>Ibid.</u>, Chapter XXIII.

8. <u>Ibid.</u>, Chapter XXI.

9. <u>Ibid.</u>

10. Josephus, <u>War</u> II.408; 433-434.

11. <u>Ibid.</u>, <u>War</u>II.499-455.

12. <u>Ibid.</u>, <u>War</u> VII. 304-406.

13. <u>Ibid.</u> <u>War</u> IV.400.

14. Yigael Yadin, <u>Masada: Herod's Fortress and the Zealots' Last Stand</u>,(New York: Random House, 1966), p. 173.

15. Geza Vermes, <u>The Dead Sea Scrolls: Qumran in Perspective</u> (Cleveland: Collins World, 1977), p. 122.

16. Burrows, p. 245.

17. Yadin, p. 172-189.

18. <u>Ibid.</u>, p. 174.

19. William R. Farmer, <u>Maccabees</u>, <u>Zealots</u>, <u>and Josephus</u>, Chapter VI.

20. Josephus, <u>War</u> II.152-153.

21. Gaster, p. 4.

47

22. <u>Ibid</u>., p. 319, #57.

23. Farmer, <u>Maccabees</u>, <u>Zealots</u>, <u>and Josephus</u>, p. 169.

24. Dupont-Sommer, p. 12-13.

25. <u>Ibid.</u>

CHAPTER IV

THE ETYMOLOGY OF ESSENE

One reason that the Essenes have remained so elusive to scholarship is that the derivation of the word Essene itself is elusive. While there have been many suggestions for an etymology, from Philo to the present day, there has been no general agreement. Some of those making suggestions derive Essene from Hebrew, others from Greek.

It has already been noted that Philo, in his Every Good Man Is Free, believes that the term Essene is a variation of ostiotes, a Greek word meaning "holiness," although he admits that the form of the Greek is inexact.[1] In all probability, Philo stretched the point because the Essenes suggested holiness to his mind. Nevertheless, Philo sensed that the origin was to be found in Greek rather than in Hebrew. The significance of this is that it would show that the name had been bestowed during the Graeco-Roman period, and that it would be the only one of the three main sects whose name was derived from the Greek. The name Pharisee comes from the Hebrew parash or the Aramaic perish. The name Sadducee means "Sons of Sadok (Zadok)."

But not everyone agrees that Essene comes from the Greek. Professor Cyrus H. Gordon, Director of the Center for Ebla Research at New York University, was the first to point out to me that some top scholars believe the word to come from the Hebrew esah, usually rendered "advice" or "counsel." Such is indeed the case. Theodor Gaster, in showing affinities between the ideas and doctrines contained in the Dead Sea Scrolls and those of early Christianity, refers to certain parallels between the Qumran community and the primitive church. "It is significant," he remarks, "...that some of the terms used to define its several constituent elements, though themselves derived from the Old Testament, possess in the Palestinian Aramaic dialect of the early Christians exactly the same quasi-technical sense as denoting parts of the ecclesiastical organization. A case in point is the term used to denote the the deliberative assembly (viz. esah); in Palestinian Aramaic...this means specifically the council of the church or synagogue...." In other words, the Essenes might have been regarded as the deliberative assembly of Judaism, or might have regarded themselves in that light. Dupont-Sommer believes that _esah_ refers to the sect as a whole and may well be the origin of _Essene_.[3]

These scholars may well be correct. The roots _es_, or _ess_, are the same. But the suffix, or second part of the word, is bothersome. Instead of Hebrew, the word _Essen_ looks like a Greek noun in the Consonant Declension ending in a liquid (the word for _Greek_ itself is one of these nouns, _'Ellen_). But in addition, the picture of the Essenes as the "deliberative council" of Judaism can hardly be an accurate representation of them if the past chapters are at all meaningful. An alternative therefore is needed.

Geza Vermes, in his study of the etymology of _Essene_,[4] noted that all etymologies of _Essene_ are controversial, and so apparently gave up the chase. He prefers the theory that they were known as "Healers" (Theraputae), thereby linking them to a group of that name in Egypt, a group with similarities to the Essenes, but also with many differences. Possibly they were a splinter group, but this has nothing to do with the term itself. In his article, Vermes actually discusses one etymology which is subscribed to here but which he rejects because he apparently ignored an important facet. Attention will be drawn to this matter as we proceed. It is an etymology which is implicit in Josephus's _Antiquities_, and it should be iterated that Josephus was a highly intelligent Jew who knew and could converse in several languages including Greek.

At one point where Josephus is describing the vestments worn by the high priest, he explains that the outer vestment was called the _ephod_, resembling the Greek _epomis_, which was the upper part of a woman's tunic fastened on the shoulder by brooches. Part of the ephod, Josephus explains, was the _essen_, a transliteration of the Hebrew word _hoshen_, apparently a kind of breastplate. The translation of _hoshen_ into Greek, Josephus adds, is _logion_,[5] a word translated into English as "oracle," although usually rendered "breastpiece of judgment" or "breastplate of judgment" in the English Bibles, perhaps in deference to those who find the word "oracle" offensive. It is of extreme importance to the layman to understand

the difference between transliteration and translation.
The Hebrew term for that part of the vestment of
a priest is transliterated into English as hoshen,
but translated as "oracle," or "breastplate," or
"breastpiece." On the other hand, if a person understood only Greek, the Hebrew term would be transliterated into Greek as "essen," but translated into
Greek as "logion." Josephus is consistent in his
use of the Greek transliteration "essen."

Josephus describes this essen in some detail
(the term essen will be used unless hoshen should
be called for). The essen, we are told had twelve
gems, all having letters graven upon them forming
the names of the sons of Jacob, the twelve tribal
chiefs, each stone having on it the name of one of
the sons. These precious stones were arranged three
to a row in four rows, and somehow in the order in
which the tribal chiefs were born.[6] This essen, with
its precious stones, fitted into the priest's vestment in a space left open at the breast, hence, presumably, the "breastpiece" of the English Bibles.

It was these precious stones which apparently
were responsible for the oracular powers of the essen,
for, according to Josephus, God, by means of the
twelve stones foreshadowed victory on the eve of
battle: "For so brilliant a light flashed out from
them (the gems) ere the army was yet in motion, that
it was evident to the whole host that God had come
to their aid. Hence it is that those Greeks who
revere our practices...call the essen logion(oracle)."[7]
It is interesting that the Essenes of Qumran called
themselves in their scrolls "The Enlightened" or
"Endowed with Insight." The group sometimes described
this illumination by the word Or-Tom - literally
"Light Perfection." This was a play on the Biblical
Urim and Thumim, parts of the ephod of the high priest.[8]

That such oracular powers were attributed to
a portion of the high priest's vestment is indeed
puzzling, for divination and diviners, or oracles,
are specifically forbidden by the Law (Deut. 18:9-14).
The Lord warned the Israelites that there should
be among them no one who practiced divination:
soothsayer, auger, sorcerer, charmer, medium, wizard,
or necromancer - an impressive list which leaves
little chance for semantic evasion. The Lord added
the information that all the above were to be found
among the nations which the Israelites were about
to invade, but the Lord's chosen were not to have

anything to do with such practices and people. Another part of the Law (Lev. 19:26) also forbids the practice, while Exodus 22:18, on a much harsher note prescribes death to any sorceress. Thus the Law is emphatically clear in forbidding the Israelites to practice divination, no matter what term might be used for it.

Yet divination was practiced by the Israelites. Whether they were unable to resist the cultural pressures of the Canaanites and other peoples of the area is difficult to say, but soon the Israelites developed their own oracles, or at least there emerged some individuals who were recognized as such. The prophets continually railed against divination but never succeeded in eradicating it. At times, too, the Israelite leaders felt the need to start a campaign to revive this part of the Law by rooting out the diviners ("sibyls" to the Greeks) and killing them. King Saul, in a moment of piety, cracked down on them, but ironically, he himself turned to the "witch" of Endor in hope that he would be given some sort of favorable prediction concerning his upcoming battle with the Philistines. (I Sam. 28:8-25).

In fact King Saul seems to have been a great believer in divination. In his campaign against the Philistines referred to in I Samuel 14, after he had discovered that his son Jonathan and his armor-bearer were missing from camp, Saul sent for the priest with his ephod, of which the hoshen was a part. Some Biblical translations render the expression "ark of God" instead of "ephod," but the Septuagint renders it "ephod," with which most scholars agree. In any case, both the ark and the ephod could be used for purposes of divining. The process of the priest's consulting the ephod, or hoshen, must have taken some time, for a great din arose among the Philistines, and Saul, impatiently, told the priest to withdraw his hand (I Sam. 14:17-19). Later, Saul again consulted the priest as to whether or not he should attack the Philistines, but no answer was received from the ephod. Interpreting this to be the result of a sin on the part of either the people or on the part of Jonathan or himself, Saul asked that, if the sin was his own or Jonathan's, the oracle of the Lord should "give Urim;" if it was the people's sin, the oracle should give "Thummin." While the exact translation of "Urim" and "Thummin' is almost an impossibility, they were apparently some kind of lots, like dice, kept in the hoshen of the ephod, their purpose to provide answers from the Lord to questions which could be answered yes or no. At any rate when Urim was given as the answer to Saul's question, indicating guilt on the part of himself or Jonathan, Saul asked for the lots to indicate which one of the two was guilty. In spite of the oracle's indicating the guilt of Jonathan, who would therefore ordinarily be put to death, this story ended happily, for Jonathan's life was redeemed in some way by the people. (I Sam. 14:36-42) These examples show clearly how deeply rooted divination and oracles were in the culture of the Israelites.

Thus, in spite of the Law, the Israelites assimilated the beliefs concerning oracles and sibyls held by neighboring peoples.[9] "Sibyl," as has been stated, was the name used by the Indo-Europeans, or Hellenes (Greeks), for diviners. Early writers seemed to have recognized only one sibyl, Sibylla by name, who was first localized at Erythrae or Cyme in Asia Minor. Strabo, the Greek geographer, noted that she went back to the most ancient times.[10] Charles Gayley suggests that Ovid's account of Sibylla's life protracted to a thousand years may be intended to represent various sibyls as being only reappearances of the same individual.[11] But at any rate, the oracles of the Greek god, Apollo, who was the twin brother of Artemis, became known as "sibyls."

Somewhat later in time, a collection of oracular prophecies appeared and gained much prestige among the Jews. These Sibylline Oracles, by which the collection is known, contained Jewish or Christian prophecies allegedly confirmed by a sibyl, but was actually the work of certain Jewish and Christian writers from c.150 BC. to c.180 AD. In these Oracles the sibyl first felt it necessary to prove her reliability, doing so by "predicting" events that had already occurred. Then she would predict future events and set forth doctrines peculiar to Hellenistic Judaism or Christianity.[12] The Oracles were held in high esteem by both Jew and non-Jew. In fact, two second-century Christian theologians thought the prophetess to be as inspired as any of the Old Testament prophets.[13]

Two historians, Josephus and Tacitus, reveal much about current belief in divination and portents in their accounts of the burning of the Temple and the destruction of Jerusalem.

53

Josephus writes at length of how the people of Jerusalem had been deluded by false prophets with tragic results, all the while ignoring the "plain warnings of God." These "plain warnings of God" consisted of a star shaped like a sword, a comet, a cow that gave birth in the Temple to a lamb, the spontaneous opening of the heavy bronze gate of the inner court, celestial armies, a voice in the Temple, and dire predictions for Jerusalem made by Jesus, son of Ananias, over a period of seven years and five months until the destruction finally occurred, and Jesus, son of Ananias, lost his life. Josephus then reflects that "God has a care for men, and by all means of premonitory signs shows His people the way to salvation, while they owe any destruction which befalls to folly and calamities of their own choosing.[14] Josephus then continues by telling how the Jews, following the destruction of the Tower of Antonia, had reduced the Temple to a square, "although they had it recorded in their oracles that the city and the sanctuary would be taken when the Temple should become four-square."[15] Another oracle found in the sacred scriptures of the Jews, Josephus adds, was ambiguous. It was prophesied that at a certain time one from their country would become ruler of the world. This, stated Josephus, incited the Jews to war, apparently believing that the Messiah was coming, but instead, the oracle in reality signified the sovereignty of Vespasian, who was proclaimed emperor on Jewish soil. So again complaining that the Jews paid no attention to God's oracles, Josephus stated that the Jews interpreted some of these portents to please themselves, others they treated with contempt, until the ruin of their country and their own destruction convinced them of their folly.[16]

Tacitus, the Roman historian, describes the fall of Jerusalem in much the same tone. At the approach of the Romans toward Jerusalem, relates Tacitus, "Contending hosts were seen meeting in the skies, arms flashed, and suddenly the Temple was illumined with fire from the clouds. Of a sudden the doors of the shrine opened and a superhuman voice cried: 'The gods are departing': at the same moment the mighty stirring of their going was heard. Few interpreted these omens as fearful; the majority firmly believed that their ancient priestly writings contained the prophecy that this was the very time when the East should grow strong and that men starting from Judea should possess the world."[17]

54

If this deeply-rooted belief in divination held by the Israelites was inherited, at least in part, from neighboring peoples, the situation was compounded by the confusion between what the Israelites regarded as true prophecy and as false prophecy. Technically, it may be said, the difference was clear. The "true" prophets always credited God with their utterances, God was speaking through them. But the "false" prophets did not credit God with their prophecies but relied upon signs or augury or conjuring up spirits. But as might be suspected, the distinction between the "true" prophet and the "false" prophet could, on certain occasions, fade to nothing. Indeed, it was an easy matter for the false prophet to credit God with any prediction he wished. The Law, however, was explicit for the Israelites: "For these nations which you are about to dispossess, give heed to soothsayers and diviners; but as for you, the Lord your God has not allowed you to do so. The Lord your God will raise up for you a prophet like me from among you, from your brethren - like him you shall heed...." (Deut. 18:14-15) But throughout their history, the Israelites continually had to be warned by true prophets to beware of false prophets, liars, and lying divination (Ez. 13:17-19; Is. 44:25 among others). Also it should be said that just as the Israelite prophets, whether true or false, credited their God with their utterances, so did the oracles of neighboring people credit their own deity with whatever information they dispensed. All magical signs and omens were merely window-dressing, although at times very impressive. The message was from the god himself, or herself. People went to consult the oracle at Delphi, for example, but there was no doubt in their minds that whatever the oracle said was a message from Apollo. The same held true for all the neighbors of the Israelites. No matter what or who the intermediary was, the message was from the deity.

Of course the intermediary in most cases was the priest, although the institution of the priesthood seemed to have attained more importance in Egypt and Palestine than it did in Greece. With the Israelites, as with others, the priesthood became the institution to relay messages from the Lord to His people, for through the covenant made with Levi, the priesthood became the mediator between Yahweh and Israel: "So shall you know that I (Yahweh, or the Lord) have sent this command to you, that my covenant with Levi may hold, says the Lord of hosts..."

(Malachi 2:04-07) Under such a covenant, it is quite understandable how a part of the vestment of a priest would include a part which was oracular in nature, for how else could a priest be a messenger between Yahweh and his People? This part of the priest's vestment was the hoshen. It is also understandable that peoples of other nations would regard the hoshen in the same way they regarded their own cult objects and vestments which served as oracles. Thus when the Greeks transliterated <u>hoshen</u> into their own language, the word became <u>essen</u> but the meaning of the translation, <u>logion</u> is translated into English as "oracle."

The word which designated the Jewish sect, then, could be derived from the Greek transliteration of <u>hoshen</u>. And it would be in no way unusual for a term used by the Jews at this time in history to have a Greek derivation. During the Hellenistic period, Greek became almost a universal language, even to such an extent that there was a need for the Old Testament to be translated into Greek, for many Jews in other countries around the shores of the East Mediterranean, especially in Egypt, had lost touch with Hebrew and even Aramaic. Thus the Greek version of the Torah was probably completed about the middle of the third century BC. Certainly a group considering itself the Elect of Israel could be designated by Greek-speaking Jews by a Greek term thought to be appropriate, in this case <u>Essen</u>, or the plural <u>Essenoi</u>.

Professor Geza Vermes examines this etymology of <u>Essenes</u> in his article "The Etymology of Essene" and rejected it for apparently two chief reasons, both based on the absence of any mention of priests. First, Josephus had stated that the essen had ceased to shine two hundred years before he had written his book, because of God's displeasure; second, Professor Vermes points out that Josephus had never mentioned any vestment. He adds what seems to be a patronizing note, that this etymology is appealing and people think the puzzle is solved, which in his judgment it is not because he believes that all the suggested etymologies are controversial.[18] It must be said, too, that Professor Vermes seems to have been incomplete in his examination, as will be shown in the appropriate place.

As far as his objections are concerned, the first cannot be taken very seriously unless one

56

accepts the supernatural. Of course the essen was not shining at the time of Josephus, nor at any other time except in the minds of the True Believers. A modern writer who submits that the essen's supernatural light was ineffectual at the time of Josephus as evidence that the Essenes did not have, or were not, priests seems to have little regard for the ordinary person's intelligence. The second objection of Professor Vermes, that Josephus never mentions vestments, again cannot be taken very seriously. There has never been the least doubt that priests were part of the Essene community. Are we then to conclude that these priests did not wear the traditional priestly vestments, including the hoshen?

The only inference one might make is that <u>all</u> Essenes were not priests and therefore did not wear priestly garb. But even here care must be taken, for under the Mosaic covenant the whole nation was to be a "kingdom of priests" and hence a holy people (Ex. 19:06). At a later date, Isaiah felt it necessary to remind the people that they were "priests of the Lord" according to the covenant (Is.61:06). Professor Raymond Abba has the following to say about the whole nation being priests: "Keeping the covenant therefore implies the consecration of the nation. Because God is holy, His people must also be holy (Lev. 11:44 f.). Also since the covenant is made with the whole nation, the existence of an official priesthood does not exclude the rest of the people from their special relationship with God."[19]

However, although all the people are priests, continues Abba, corporate responsibility must of necessity be delegated to representative persons, who discharge it on the behalf of the community as a whole. Hence in public and national worship, the priests act as representatives of the people. To perform this duty, a three-fold hierarchy of priests was formed, culminating in the high priest, in whom the vicarious sanctity of the priesthood is gathered up. By bearing the names of the twelve tribes of Israel on the essen, he represents the people as a whole (Ex. 28:29).[20]

Thus the Essenes, considering themselves to be the true Congregation of Israel and adhering strictly to the Law, would regard themselves as priests under the Mosaic covenant but designated the "Sons of Zadok" to represent them as the priesthood. The "Sons of Zadok" were the descendants of

Levi and were the foremost priestly family at the time of David. They were also the ones whom the prophet Ezekiel had designated, in his vision of the restored Temple, as the only legitimate priests (Ez. 40:46; 44:15; 48:11).

Theodor Gaster has the following to say about how the Qumran Community, its teachers and priests, regarded itself: "It (the Community) was not waiting to receive the Law; it already possessed it. Its aim was simply to assert the Law, to deliver it from the realm of darkness in which it had become engulfed. The Torah - that is, the Divine Teaching (or Guidance) as revealed to Moses had, it was maintained, been successively garbled and perverted by 'false expositors.' The Community's main purpose was to exemplify and promulgate the true interpretation. It based that interpretation on a kind of 'apostolic succession,' begun by the prophets and continued by a series of inspired leaders each of whom was known as 'the correct expositor' or 'right teacher' (not Teacher of Righteousness, as many scholars have rendered it)- that is, the orthodox expounder of the Word. The 'right teacher' was probably in every case a priest, his title being derived from Moses' farewell blessing upon the tribe of Levi: 'They have observed Thy word and kept Thy covenant. They shall teach Jacob Thine ordinances, and Israel Thy Law'" (Deut. 33:09-10).[21]

In a note Gaster succinctly gives his reasons for stating that the "right teachers" were undoubtedly priests: "First, only a priest would have had uncontested authority so to lay down the law. Second, our documents (the Qumran scrolls) say specifically, over and over again, that the rules and standards of the community were determined of old by the 'sons of Zadok, the priests.' Third, the Manual of Discipline affirms expressly that 'the priests alone are to have authority in all judicial and economic matters.' Fourth, the Prophetic Teacher who will arise at the end of the present era and usher in the Messianic Age is invariably associated in Jewish tradition with either Elijah, Phinehas, or even Melchizedek, all of whom were priests."[22] Elijah and Phinehas, it will be remembered, have been singled out as men of zeal, ancestors of the Essenes. There seems little room for doubt that priests played an important role in the life of the Essenes, and these priests must have worn the traditional priestly garb, which, of course, included the hoshen as part of the ephod.

But a person might ask why, since all priests wore the ephod with its hoshen, should the Essenes be singled out by the hoshen alone. The obvious answer is that in all likelihood, the priests of the Essenes were especially known for their prophecy, as they would phrase it, or even the general members of the group might have been known for predictions.

In this matter, Josephus is again very helpful. There were some Essenes, according to the historian, who were well known for their ability to predict the future. Moreover, these particular Essenes were not of the official priesthood. Perhaps the Essenes believed more strictly that part of the Mosaic covenant which holds that Yahweh considered all Israel to be priests than did other Jews. At any rate, Josephus states that "There are among them (the Essenes) who profess to foretell the future, being versed from their early years in holy books, various forms of purfication and apophthegms of prophets; and seldom, if ever, do they err in their predictions."[23] This statement of Josephus is a most interesting one, for the implication understood is that the predictions of the prophets and those of the diviners were of a different nature, which they were. Raymond Abba defines the difference. "Whereas the revelatory experience of the prophet was personal and direct, that of the priest was collective and mediated, either through divination or through his training and accumulated knowledge of the past."[24]

In referring to the ability and repute of the Essenes in predicting the future, Josephus specified three cases, and in none of the cases is the Essene a traditional priest. One individual was not only able to predict, but also gave instructions in predicting to disciples and companions. Such a story strongly suggests that the Essenes in general, not only their priests, indulged in the practice of divination. This oracle who held the classes in divining was an Essene by the name of Judas, who, according to Josephus, had never been known to speak falsely. A story told by Josephus about Judas the Essene is not without a certain grim irony. It seems that Aristobulus I, the Hasmonean monarch, in the course of events, killed most of his own family. But his brother, Antigonus, he loved dearly. Judas the Essene predicted that Antigonus would die on a certain day at Straton's Tower, but on the designated

day, as Judas was speaking to his disciples and
friends, he happened to see a person who he thought
was Antigonus passing the temple. The diviner was
greatly upset, for the place where he had predicted
Antigonus would be killed was approximately 65 miles
distant, and since most of the day was already spent,
it seemed that Judas had predicted falsely. Lamenting
his error, the diviner called for his own life for
having done so. But in the next moment word came
that Antigonus had been murdered at Straton's Tower,
just as Judas had predicted. Thus the oracular powers
of Judas were vindicated and his record for having
never predicted falsely remained intact. Because
there was no need now for Judas to forfeit his life,
there must have been a great deal of joy and thank-
fulness, not only on the part of Judas but his followers as well - all at the expense of poor Antigonus.
Josephus tells this story with what must have been
a straight face, apparently with no recognition of
the possibility of irony in the situation, no matter
how grim.[25]

Another Essene who was known for his divining,
according to Josephus, was a man by the name of Simon.
The story related about this Essene had to do with
a dream by Archelaus, the governor of Judea, and
is reminiscent of the story in Genesis concerning
the interpretation of the pharaoh's dream by Joseph.
In his dream Archelaus saw oxen browsing on nine
tall and full-grown ears of corn. After many soothsayers had given their interpretation of the dream,
Archelaus remained unsatisfied and sent for Simon
the Essene. Simon told Archelaus that the ears of
corn denoted years, while the oxen designated a
revolution, because they turned over the soil while
browsing. Simon told the governor that the true
interpretation was that he, Archelaus, would reign
for as many years as there were ears of corn but
would die following some revolutionary events. The
time element in the story is somewhat confusing,
but apparently Archelaus ruled for nine years, when
he was banished by Caesar to Vienna.[26]

The third reference by Josephus to the remarkable
ability of the Essenes to foretell the future con-
cerned a very virtuous Essene by the name of Manaemus
(Menahem in Hebrew). According to the story, when
Herod was just a boy on the way to his teacher,
Manaemus greeted him as "king of the Jews" and at
the same time slapped the future king on his backside.
After some words of wisdom for the young Herod,

Manaemus took his leave, ostensibly making little impression on the boy. But in later years after he had become king, Herod recalled the incident and sent for Manaemus and asked as to the length of time he would reign. Manaemus was most reluctant to answer, but when pressed, gave a reply which apparently satisfied the king. Josephus claims that from that time on, Herod held all Essenes in honor.[27]

Thus, if Josephus is to be believed, the Essenes placed great emphasis upon, and were noted for, divination. It does seem strange that these Essenes, noted for their piety, should at the same time indulge in a practice explicitly forbidden by the Law, even though divination had been practiced especially by the priests for hundreds of years. Nevertheless, in a Graeco-Roman culture, it would not seem unlikely for a Jewish sect, well-known for their diviners, to become identified with the part of the priests' vestments having to do with prediction, the hoshen, or essen. The group would then become "Essenoi," or "Those of the essen."

It will be recalled that Professor Vermes considered this etymology and rejected it for two reasons which, from this point of view, do not seem serious. Perhaps he would have reconsidered if he had pursued the matter a little farther. He neglected to notice, apparently, that in addition to essen being a transliteration of the Hebrew hoshen, the transliteration itself is a Greek word. For example, when the Hebrew word is transliterated into English, the result is hoshen, but there is no such word in the English vocabulary. We are merely trying, as far as it is possible, to put the Hebrew sounds into the English alphabet. But when the Hebrew word is transliterated into Greek, the transliteration is a Greek word which has two meanings. First, it refers to a priest of the East Mediterranean goddess, Artemis. The second meaning is "king-bee."

Thus it would be quite natural for Hellenized people in that part of the world, including Jews, to use the word Essenoi, "Essenes" or "Those of the essen," to refer to that Jewis sect which was noted for divination, since a portion of their priests' vestment, what they called the essen was so closely connected with prediction. It would be much more understandable if there was some connection in persons' minds between the sect and priests of Artemis. Or with bees. The use of "Essenes" to identify the sect, if such a connection existed, would of necessity be a derogatory epithet and would explain why the sectarians never used the word to refer to themselves.

Ruins of the buildings of the Essene Community, known as Khirbet Qumran, overlooking the Dead Sea

NOTES TO CHAPTER IV

1. Philo, _Every Good Man Is Free_. 75.

2. Gaster, p. 18.

3. Dupont-Sommer, p. 43.

4. Geza Vermes, "The Etymology of Essenes," _Revue de Qumran 7_, June 1960.

5. Josephus, _Antiquities_, III.163.

6. _Ibid._, 166-169.

7. _Ibid._ 216.

8. Gaster, p. 21.

9. See my _Bronze Age Civilization: The Philistines and the Danites_ (Washington, D.C.: Public Affairs Press, 1975).

10. Strabo, _Geography_ 14.34.

11. Charles, Gayley, _Classic Myths_. Rev. ed. (Boston: Ginn, 1939), p. 533.

12. "Sibylline Oracles," _Encyclopaedia Britannica_, Encyclopaedia Brittanica, Inc.: Chicago, 1977.

13. _Ibid._

14. Josephus, _War_, VI.288-311.

15. _Ibid._, 311.

16. _Ibid._, 315.

17. Tacitus, _Histories_ (Loeb Classical Lib. ed., Cambridge: Harvard, 1969. Book V,XIII.

18. Vermes, "The Etymology of Essene."

19. Raymond Abba, "Priests and Levites," _The Interpreter,s Dictionary of the Bible_.

20. _Ibid._

21. Gaster, p. 5.

22. Ibid., p. 29-30.

23. Josephus, War II.159.

24. Abba, "Priests and Levites."

25. Josephus, Antiquities, XIII.311-313.

26. Ibid., War, II.112-113.

27. Ibid., Antiquities XV.373-378.

CHAPTER V

MILK AND HONEY AS DIVINE SUBSTANCES
IN THE EAST MEDITERRANEAN AREA

It may seem that a discussion of milk and honey, as well as the animals which produce them, in the East Mediterranean area would be leading a reader far afield from the Jewish Essenes, especially if the discussion leads to a consideration of pagan deities known especially in the Hellenic world. But when the Hebrew <u>hoshen</u> is transliterated into Greek as <u>essen</u>, which is also an actual Greek word meaning "king-bee" or designating a priest of Artemis and when it is further suggested that the name of the Jewish sect "Essenes" may very well be derived from that Greek word, an examination into the matter becomes not only relevant but essential. One tends to forget how close were the cultural relationships between and among the peoples of the Aegeo-Mediterranean area. The sea was a highway rather than a barrier. Some years ago Professor Cyrus H. Gordon, presently the Director of the Center for Ebla Research at New York University, insisted repeatedly that studies of ancient Semitic and Indo-European civilizations should not be compartmentalized, that even during the Bronze Age close relationships existed between Egyptians, Hebrews, Ugarit-speaking peoples, Phoenicians, Minoans, Hittites, Hellenes, and others. In fact, the relationships were so close among all these peoples that Professor Gordon used the word <u>ecumene</u> to identify the whole Aegeo-East Mediterranean community.[1]

While the emphasis will shift in this chapter away from Judea, it is well to remember that in the Old Testament reference is made so often to Canaan as the Promised Land flowing with milk and honey, the expression has tended over the years to become trite. What is not so well-known, however, is that Egypt also is described as a land flowing with milk and honey (Num. 16:13). It is indeed strange that Egypt, the land of oppression for the Hebrews, should be described by the same expression as that used for the Promised Land, Canaan. It is interesting, too, that this expression is used for both Canaan and Egypt in the same Book of the Pentateuch. The

probable explanation is that the expreession is a
figurative one, not literal. This probability is
strengthened when it is considered that neither Egypt
nor Canaan could hardly be thought of as a "land
of plenty," a meaning commonly associated with the
expression. Moreover, milk was not commonly drunk
by the Hebrews; rather it was made into cheese and
curds. In addition, all over the Aegeo-Mediterranean
area, milk and honey were regarded as divine substances, so that the meaning of the expression might
be rendered "a land blessed by the gods," or something similar. The Hebrews, then, would have thought
of Canaan as "a land blessed by Yahweh, our God."
Egypt, of course, would have been under the aegis
of the Egyptian gods.

Jane Harrison, in her Prolegamena to the Study
of Greek Religion, discusses the background and
meaning of milk and honey in Greek religion, especially
in Orphism, maintaining that they were a holdover
from the Nephalia, a libation made without wine to
the deities of the lower world, a practice before
Dionysos "took possession of the vine." Thus the
libation consisted of either water and honey or milk
and honey, honey never being omitted. But although
this libation, the Nephalia, was reserved mostly
for the chthonic, or underworld, gods, the libation
was also observed at Athens, whose deities were
associated mainly with the upper regions, and the
Athenians, always careful in such matters, brought
only sober offerings. One may recall the unfortunate
Oedipus. During the course of his blind wandering,
he was bidden to make atonement for having unwittingly violated the sacred grove of the underworld
deities. The chorus directed him to first make a
libation from the sacred spring and then, facing
the dawn, to pour the libation on the earth. After
pouring it, he was to fill the urn with water and
honey.

The Nephalia, then, consisted of offerings of
milk and honey used in the rites of Orphism. To
the Orphic, states Harrison, there was a sacred symbolism connected with the kid and milk. Even one
of the titles of Dionysos was Eriphos (Kid), suggesting
something divine about this animal. The initiate
of Orphism, she continues, believed himself to be
new-born as a young animal, as a kid, one of the
god's many incarnations; and as a kid, as part of
the ritual, he falls into milk. Thus the Epiphany
of Dionysos was shown not only by wine but by milk

and honey.[4]

The concept of milk and honey as divine substances was not only widespread but also long-lasting. According to Harrison, it can be perceived in the primitive rites of the Christian Church. In the primitive Church, she explains, the Sacrament of Baptism was immediately followed by Communion, the custom still being observed among the Copts. The neophyte drank not only of the wine but also a cup of milk and honey mixed - those "newborn in Christ" partaking of the food of babes. Since that time the Church has severed Baptism from Communion and lost the symbolism of milk and honey.[5] Perhaps St. Jerome was responsible for the change, for he noted that much of what was done in the Church of his time did not have the sanction of Holy Writ, among the unsanctioned rites, the cup of milk and honey. Harrison vouches for the pagan origin of the rite by quoting a prescription taken from one of the magic papyri in which the worshipper is thus instructed: "Take the honey with the milk, drink of it before the rising of the sun, and there shall be in thy heart something that is divine." Harrison states that "The milk and honey can be materialized into a future 'happy land' flowing with milk and honey, but the promise of the magical papyrus is the utmost possible guerdon of present spiritual certainty."[6]

The prescription of a mixture of milk and honey is reminiscent of an event recorded in I Samuel 14, except that here only honey is mentioned. In a campaign against the Philitines, Saul had given orders that none of his army was to eat anything until evening, when he expected the Philistines to have been defeated. Saul's son, Jonathan, however, had not been informed of the order, and when he came upon some honey in the forest, he took some and ate it. We are then told that his eyes were "enlightened" (KJV) or "became bright"(RSV). Jonathan's "bright eyes" must have revealed something divine in his heart. He revealed this to his hungry men before they went into battle against the Philistines, and apparently as a result, defeated their enemies soundly.

Any attempt to trace the domesticating of bees is bound to be frustrating. References to bees and honey are found in the most ancient literature from Egypt to the land of the Hittites, to India, and even to Siberia. Honey was renowned as a food and delicacy, as sugar was as yet unknown, and thus there is evidence that bees were domsticated at a very early period so that men were better able to control the supply of honey, as well as wax, another valuable product of bees. The early Law Code of the Hittites, for example, states that "If anyone steals bees in a swarm, formerly they used to give one mina of silver, (but) now he shall give five sheckles of silver."[7] This statement implies not only that bees were domesticated in this ancient society, but that the practice had been carried on for some time, for apparently bee-stealing had been on the increase. Laws concerning bees are also found in other ancient literature such as the Vedas of India.

The high esteem in which honey was held was practically universal, peoples everywhere prizing it. Strabo and Pausanias, two early geographers, both attest to this fact and then add their personal preference as to where the best honey could be found. Strabo mentioned the quality of honey in locales from Europe to Asia, the best, in his judgment, coming from Sicily.[8] According to the taste of Pausanias, however, the best pastures for bees were the Attic mountains of Greece, with the exception of the country of the Alzones, a people of southern Russia.[9] The Israelites also valued honey highly as we can judge from the many references to it in the Old Testament. It is noteworthy that the Essenes themselves kept bees, and it was the task of some members of the community to superintend the swarms.[10] It is of more than passing interest that Philo singles out only the Essenes for raising bees.

The ancients placed such great value on bees that they were often assigned magical powers sometimes expressed figuratively in their tales. Pausanias, for example, in describing a section of Thebes, points out Pindar's tomb and then relates the story of how Pindar, on his way home one day, became tired and lay down to rest. Bees alighted on him and plastered his lips with wax, thus accounting for Pindar's career as a poet.[11] The same idea is expressed in much the same way by the lover in the Song of Solomon: "Your lips distil nectar, my bride; honey and milk are under your tongue." And again the same idea in the Psalms to describe the words of Yahweh: "sweeter also than honey and dripping of the honeycomb (19:10).

The magical powers attributed to bees also included giving portents. In a tale similar to the

one concerning Pindar, Pliny relates how bees alighted
on the mouth of Plato when the philosopher was still
an infant,[12]"portending the charm of that matchless
eloquence."[12] Pliny also relates that bees alighted
in the camp of General Drusus on the occasion of
the battle that he was to win at Arbalo. Pliny hinted,
however, that this was an exceptional case, for the
augers invariably thought of such an event as a
direful portent.[13]

Related to magical powers were the many medicinal
and health-giving properties attributed to bees and
honey. Bee stings as a remedy for arthritis covers
the whole span of history to even the present day.
Pliny compiled a long list of uses for honey, from
keeping a body from decaying to use as a treatment
for pneumonia. And mixed[14] with water or wine, it
was considered a panacea.[14] Robert Graves informs
us of a more revolting medicinal use: throughout
the East Mediterranean area, a remedy for sick[15] children
was to swallow a mouse coated with honey.[15] It is
hoped that this was one of the more desperate remedies
after others had failed.

Keeping a body from decaying by placing it in
honey was a common custom throughout the area. To
be returned from Babylon, the body of Alexander the
Great, who had died there, was preserved by this
method.[16] Likewise the body of the Spartan king,
Agesipolis, who was killed while conducting a war
against some northern neighbors, was placed in honey
until it could be returned to Sparta.[17] Also, in his
Antiquities, Josephus relates how King Aristobulus
was poisoned by followers of Pompey, and his body
lay preserved in honey until Antony finally sent
it back to Judea.[18] Diodorus Siculus also makes a
report of another Spartan general who had died far
from home. Agesilaus, he relates, following a victory
over the Egyptians, was on his way back to Greece
when he died and his body preserved by packing it
in honey.[19] The scholiast of Diodorus points out that
this account differs from Plutarch's, which states
that the body of Agesilaus was enclosed in wax because
no honey was available, but such a difference is
of little consequence, since wax is also a product
of bees.

It is not known whether this practice of pre-
serving a body in honey was extended to the common
people, for history for the most part seems to center
around kings and others of high rank. Still it can

be inferred that at least some people at the time believed in an after-life and that this after-life would continue in much the same way as the earthly one had. It would seem to follow, then, that honey, which was used to preserve the body, would come to be regarded over a period of time as leading to immortality. Such a concept may be perceived as far back as Homer. In his _Iliad_, the poet relates how Achilles, before arraying himself for battle against the Trojan prince, Hector, confessed to his mother, the goddess Thetis, that he was afraid that the body of his slain friend, Patroclos, would become "prey to flies and worms." To console her son, Thetis then shed ambrosia and nectar through the nostrils of Patroclos so the flesh would remain sound as it had been in life.[20] Such an incipient concept of immortality is revealed also in a sepulchral inscription cited by Jane Harrison:

Here lies Boethus Muse-bedewed, undying
Joy hath he of sweet sleep in honey lying.[21]

From this sepulchral inscription it thus seems clear, as Harrison puts it, that honey used in ancient days to embalm the dead became the symbol of eternal bliss.

However, all concepts of the after-life were not quite so blissful. It was a belief, common in the region, that while the after-life was an extension of the earthly one (a belief not greatly improved upon in the twentieth century), it was hardly a happy one. Odysseus, it may be remembered, was required to make a journey to the land of the dead, where he conversed with relatives and friends who had already died, and although these shades were most unhappy, Odysseus was able to recognize them as they had appeared in life. The picture that Homer paints of this after-life is a dark and fearful one.[22] The shade of Achilles reflects this unhappiness when he replies to Odysseus, "Nay, seek not to speak soothingly to me of death, glorious Odysseus. I should choose, so I might live on earth, to serve as the hireling of another, of some portionless man whose livelihood was but small, rather to be lord over all the dead that have perished."[23] The other shades appeared just as unhappy as Achilles. It must be confessed, however, that Homer seems somewhat ambivalent when elsewhere he refers to the Elysian plain, where "life is easiest for men."[24] Possibly the theological concept of heaven and hell go far back in time.

The Egyptians had somewhat similar views, but nowhere do we find people so preoccupied with death and the preparation for the life to come. This preoccupation seems to have touched most phases of their culture, and the many material objects found in tombs to keep the deceased one happy in his after-life have been well publicized. In recent years, the treasures taken from the tomb of Tutankhamun have become familiar to people in many parts of the world, thanks to the generosity of the Egyptian government in lending these amazing funerary objects to museums in a number of countries. And when it is remembered that Tutankhamun was only a minor pharaoh, one can only guess as to the riches that went into the tombs of major pharaohs to keep them happy in the next world. Every attempt was made to see that nothing would be lacking in the next life that the person possessed in his earthly exist-ence. It is obvious, however, that the grave-robbers who dispossessed the dead pharaohs of these riches did not stand in so much awe and fear of the ruler's power after death as did their ancestors while the monarch was living.

But while there were similarities between Greek and Egyptian concepts of the after-life, Egyptians had quite complex ideas concerning souls. While "after-life" and "soul" are perhaps not synonymous, they are closely related. The Egyptians believed that both gods and humans had souls, not only one, but a number. It was believed, for example, that the soul of a god took the form of an animal and was regarded as the Ba soul. Thus many deities of Egypt were identified in the form of some animal: Amon, a ram or having a ram's head; Anubis, a jackal or male figure having the head of a jackal or dog; Bast, a cat; Sabet, a crocodile; Horus, a falcon; and there were others. These animals being sacred, of course received special care. Strabo tells of a sacred crocodile at Arsinoe, which, he said, had earlier been called "Crocodeiloupolis" in honor of the beast. It was fed by priests with meat and wine and a honey mixture.[25]

The Egyptians believed that men and gods also possessed a Ka soul. In rites connected with mum-mification, honey was used, for the person's Ka had to be fed after death and the bee was believed to be the Ka; thus the soul took the form of a bee. The gods also possessed a Ka soul. Each pharaoh believed himself to be the son of the solar deity,

Re, and it is a matter of more than casual interest that the bee was used as the hieroglyphic symbol for the king of Lower Egypt from 3500 BC. for about 4000 years,[26] and the hieroglyph for the king of Upper Egypt was a variation. Since the symbol for the pharaoh was a bee, it would be natural to think of his <u>Ka</u> and those of his subjects as bees, with the pharaoh's a kind of king-bee.

The Greeks referred to Zeus at times in the same way, as King-bee, "Essen." In the hymn by Callimachus to Zeus, the poet sings, "Thou (Zeus) wert made sovereign of the gods..."[27] or at least this is the translation by A.W. Mair. But the Greek expression in the text is <u>theon essena</u>, and thus the passage may, or should, be translated "Thou wert made King-bee of the gods...", for the <u>Etymologicum Magnum</u> has the translation of <u>essen</u> as "king-bee." It is interesting that the Ephesian Artemis in all probability was called "Queen-bee" and her priests, "Essenoi" or "King-bees."

John Chadwick, who was the associate of the late Michael Ventris in deciphering the Minoan Linear B tablets, indicates how important honey was in the life and religion of the Mycenaeans (the name given to the predominant inhabitants of Greece during the latter half of the second millennium BC.). The title "bee-keeper," he states, appears among the land-tenure documents, and several people held leases from him, suggesting that he was a person of some importance. Others of less importance bore a title which combines the word for honey with a word like "overseer" or "chief."[28] This title of "Bee-keeper" was common around the area and always carried with it religious connotations. Chadwick further explains that the chief context in which honey appears in the Linear B tablets also was religious. He relates how a series of tablets found at Knossos on Crete show large jars of honey being sent as offerings to various deities. Another group of these documents from Knossos with religious associations were known as the "honey tablets" in which the name of Eileithuia, the goddess of childbirth, is mentioned.[29] It is of some significance that she later became identified with Artemis, whose symbol at Ephesus was a bee and whose priests were Essenes, king-bees.

Among the Israelites, the concept of the afterlife is quite similar to those of other peoples of the area. In the Old Testament, the place is referred

of the Greeks even at the time of Homer. He was becoming the god not only of the _aither_, but of the whole earth including the underworld, that part of the universe farthest from the _aither_. Almost a thousand years later, Pausanias, in describing the temple of the Olympian Zeus at Athens, noted that Hadrian, the Roman emperor, dedicated both the temple and the statue. Inside the precincts, he continues, are a bronze Zeus, a temple of Cronos and Rhea, and an enclosure of Earth surnamed "Olympian." Here, he states the floor opens and every year there is cast into it wheat meal mixed with honey.[42]

Other epithets linked Zeus to the earth by means of honey or bees. The Greek word for honey is _meli_, while the word for bee is _melissa_. Thus the 'king-bee" of the gods, Zeus, was referred to as Zeus _Melissaios_, "Zeus of the Bees," a possible allusion to the birth story.[43] He was also known as _Zeus Meli-Genitor_, "Zeus, Producer of Honey."[44]

There is another story connected with the birth of Zeus on Crete which is of some interest. According to this story, there was a Cretan king by the name of Melisseus, "Honey-Man," who had two daughters. Rhea, the mother of Zeus, committed the care of the infant to the two daughters. Ernest Neustadt, in a dissertation early in the century, notes that the two daughters were named Amaltheia and Melissa, the former feeding Zeus on milk and Melissa feeding him on honey. By this deed Melissa was established as the first honey-priestess of the Great Mother.[45] These honey-priestesses were associated with many of the earth deities and will be discussed in a later chapter.

One other chthonian aspect of Zeus would be appropriate to mention, since the Essenes were so well-known for their oracular powers: Zeus as Oracle. In the East Mediterranean area, the early oracles were delivered by the Earth-goddess. Robert Graves indicates that the power of these oracles was considered so great that the patriarchal invaders from the north made a practice of seizing the shrines and either appointing "interpreters" or retaining those who had been there.[46] The invaders apparently wanted to take no chances with the native oracles.

The first oracle of the Greeks, according to ancient writers, was that of Zeus at Dodona. This oracle was supposed to go back to the Pelasgians, the original inhabitants of the Greek peninsula, and belonged to the cult of the oak tree, in which the god was supposed to dwell.[47] It was apparently one of those oracles taken over by the invaders from the north. Homer mentions this oracle, describing the priests as "those with unwashen feet that couch on the ground."[48] This suggests worshippers or servants of a chthonian power of a time far earlier than Homer.

Those priests described as having "unwashen feet" who slept on the ground were males, according to Homer, but by the time of the historian, Herodotus (5th century BC.), Zeus had acquired female diviners, or priestesses, at Dodona. The historian relates one of his stories told him by priests of Zeus in Egyptian Thebes. Two priestesses had been carried away from Thebes by Phoenicians, one being sold in Libya, and the other in Hellas, and the latter was supposed to have been the founder of divination in that country.[49] It seems, then, when the invaders took over the oracle at Dodona, it requires relatively little time to replace the male diviners with females.

One of the foremost oracles, according to the ancients, was Trophonios, whose site was located at Lebadeia, where he was referred to as Zeus Trophonios. This is known by an inscription at the site of his shrine.[50] According to Pausanias, the Boeotians learned about Trophonios from the Pythian priestess at Delphi, who instructed them to go to Lebadeia to consult Trophonios. The Boeotians at first could not find the oracle, but a swarm of bees appeared, and one of the envoys followed them until they went into the ground. He followed and found the oracle, who then taught him the ritual and observances. In describing the ceremony, Pausanias pictures Trophonios as a serpent to be fed with honey cakes.[51]

It is most interesting that Zeus was associated with or depicted as a snake in other cults, especially when he was worshipped as Zeus Meilikios - Meilikios, the Gentle or Gracious One, Easy to be Entreated or Propitiated. Jane Harrison discusses Zeus Meilikios in connection with the festival called "Diasia,"[52] and it is a most significant discussion.

According to Harrison, the ancestral ritual of Zeus Meilikios included a holocaust of pigs, that is, the burnt sacrifice of whole pigs, and the god himself was regarded as a source of wealth, a kind of Ploutos.[53] Two matters concerning this holocaust

78

of pigs are noteworthy. First, the ritual was entirely alien to the Zeus of Homer, the Zeus of the <u>aither</u>, who preferred his food in small pieces. Thus the fusion between the deity of the invaders and that of the native inhabitants had already been in progress. Second, it raises the question as to whether Meilikios was the cult of Zeus prescribed in the Temple at Jerusalem by Antiochus Epiphanes, for we are told that swine were offered to Zeus on the altar in the Temple, one of the acts which sparked the Maccabean uprising. It is stated elsewhere (2 Macc. 6:2) that the orders of Antiochus were to dedicate the temple to Olympian Zeus, and it may be recalled that in the temple of Olympian Zeus at Athens, there was an enclosure of earth, and every year there was cast into it meal mixed with honey, showing the chthonic character of Zeus just as the sacrifice of the swine did. One of the propitiatory offerings to Zeus Meilikios was <u>meilikia</u>, honey mixed in the offering.

Harrison also refers to six reliefs, which she has reproduced in her volume. One shows the inscription "To Zeus Meilikios" above a coiled serpent, indicating that at the place where the relief had been found, Zeus had been worshipped as a snake. Another relief shows worshippers presenting themselves before the snake-god, with the inscription "Aristarche to Zeus Meilikios." Harrison states "It is not that Zeus the Olympian has an 'underworld aspect;' it is the cruder fact that he of the upper air, of the thunder and lightning, extrudes an ancient serpent-demon of the lower world, Meilichios."[54]

Harrison continues with the other reliefs on which the serpent-god is depicted. Then in her final relief, Meilikios is a snake no longer but a human, although still an earth-god. He bears the cornucopia and his victim is the pig. Harrison concludes this portion of her discussion: "By the light, then, of these reliefs the duality, the inner discrepancy of Zeus Meilichios admits of a simple and straight-forward conclusion. It is the monument of a super-position of cults."[55]

This was the Zeus, then, that the Jews of the Graeco-Roman period knew so well. By the superposition of cultures he had ceased to be just the god of the <u>aither</u> but had become chthonian as well, associated with the divine animal, the bee, and its equally divine product, honey. It was also the Zeus whose altar was to be erected in the Temple at Jerusalem and who was to be offered swine's flesh there, igniting the rebellion of men of zeal.

The durability of the chthonic religions of the East Mediterranean is attested to by their influence on that which came with the Indo-Europeans from the north. It is most remarkable that the culture of the israelies, itself having its roots in the East Mediterranean area, could resist the religions of their neighbors as well as they did. But they were never entirely successful. Both Jew and Christian bear the marks of battle even today.

Cave on Mount Dikte in Crete that tradition identifies as the birthplace of Zeus. Another tradition had Zeus born in a cave on Mount Ida. Archaeological evidence has unearthed sanctuaries to the god at both sites.

NOTES TO CHAPTER V

1. See Cyrus H. Gordon, The Ancient Near East. (New York: Norton, 1965. His other books reflect the same basic philosophy.

2. Jane Harrison, Prolegomena to the Study of Greek Religion (New York: Meridian Books, 1960),508-509.

3. Sophocles, Oedipus at Colonus (Loeb Classical Library, Cambridge: Harvard, 1968) 466-485.

4. Harrison, p. 595.

5. Ibid., p. 596.

6. Ibid., p. 596-597.

7. O.R. Gurney, The Hittites (Boston: D.C. Heath, 1954), p. 81.

8. Strabo 6.2.7.

9. Pausanias, Description of Greece (Loeb Classical Library, Cambridge: Harvard, 1964) "Attica" xxxii.1

10. Philo, Hypothetica 11.8.

11. Pausanias, "Boeotia" XXIII.2.

12. Pliny, XI.xviii.55.

13. Ibid.

14. Ibid.

15. Robert Graves, The Greek Myths, 2 Vol. (New York: New American Library, 1959), Vol. 1, p. 306-307.

16. "Embalming," Encyclopaedia Britannica.

17. J.B. Bury, A History of Greece (New York: The Modern Library, n.d.), p. 544.

18. Josephus, Antiquities XIV.124.

19. Diodorus Siculus (Loeb Classical Library,

Cambridge: Harvard, 1963) XV.93.6

20. Homer, The Iliad (Loeb Classical Library, Cambridge: Harvard, 1963) XIX.35

21. Harrison, p. 595.

22. Homer, The Odyssey (Loeb Classical Library, Cambridge: Harvard, 1966) Books XI and XIV.

23. Ibid., XI.489-490.

24. Ibid., IV. 564.565.

25. Strabo, 17.1.38.

26. Hilda M. Ransome, The Sacred Bee (Boston: Houghton Mifflin, 1937), p. 24.

27. Callimachus, Hymns and Epigrams (Loeb Classical Library, Cambridge: Harvard, 1969), Hymn I.65.

28. John Chadwick, The Mycenaean World (Cambridge: Cambridge University Press, 1976), p. 125-126.

29. Ibid., p. 98.

30. R.F. Schnell, "Rephaim," The Interpreter's Dictionary of the Bible.

31. In the Septuagint, the reference is Proverbs 6:08.

32. W.K.C. Guthrie, The Greeks and Their Gods (Boston: Beacon Press, 1951), Chapters VIII and IX.

33. Martin Nilsson, The Minoan-Mycenaean Religion and Its Survival in Greek Religion (New York: Biblo and Tannen, 1971).

34. R.E. Witt, Isis in the Graeco-Roman World (Ithaca: Cornell, 1971), p. 130.

35. Homer, The Iliad, XV.185-195.

36. Diodorus Siculus, V.70.

37. Nilsson, p. 544.

38. Diodorus Siculus, V.70.

39. Nilsson, p. 543.

40. Hesiod (Loeb Classical Library, Cambridge: Harvard, 1964), Works and Days 465.

41. Homer, The Iliad IX.457.

42. Pausanias, "Attica," xviii.7.

43. A.B. Cook, Zeus: A Study in Ancient Religions (New York: Biblo and Tannen, 1965), Vol. III, p. 1112.

44. From a Greek papyrus in the British Museum.

45. Ernest Neustadt, De Iove Cretico (Berlin: Mayer and Muller, 1906), p. 144.

46. Graves, I, p. 181.

47. Strabo, 7.7.10.

48. Homer, The Iliad, XVI.235.

49. Herodotus (Loeb Classical Library, Cambridge: Harvard, 1966), II.54.

50. Guthrie, p. 219.

51. Pausanias, "Boeotia" xl.1-2.

52. Harrison, p. 23.

53. Ibid., p. 15.

54. Ibid., p. 19.

55. Ibid., p. 21.

The great Mother of the gods, Kybele, of Phrygia.
As Earth-Mothers, she and the Ephesian Artemis
were believed to possess similar functions
in the fertility and fructification of nature
and humans.

CHAPTER VI

ARTEMIS

It has been seen that honey and honey, as well as milk, were sacred objects among the peoples of the East Mediterranean and were included in the worship and rites of many of their deities. At least some of the great Earth-Mothers of the area were known as "Queen-Bees," including Artemis of Ephesus, who counted in her retinue priests known as Essenes, or King-Bees. The Ephesian Artemis at one time or another was associated with other goddesses, including, very strangely, one from the north who also became known as Artemis by the Hellenes, but whose characteristics and functions were often quite different from those of the Ephesian.

This northern deity of the Hellenes was a virgin goddess, one of modesty and maidenly vigor. As Apollo, her twin brother, was noted as an archer, so indeed was Artemis. In Homer, women who died suddenly and without pain were said to have been slain by her _agave belea_, gentle darts, as men were slain by the arrows of Apollo. It was thought that the moon's arc was her bow, and its beams her arrows, for at one time she was identified with Selene, the moon-goddess. As a virgin, Artemis likewise imposed a vow of chastity on her nymphs, and she was swift and sure in her punishment of any who might slip, but ironically, she helped women in childbirth. She was well known as goddess of the chase, but again ironically, she was the guardian of both wild and domestic beasts. Homer referred to her as _potnia theron_, "mistress" or "queen" of wild animals.

But this modest and chaste Artemis of the early Hellenes bore little resemblance to the Artemis who was found dominating the whole Mediterranean area upon the arrival of the Hellenes in that part of the world. This pre-Hellenic Artemis, whose worship was centered at Ephesus, could not have been more dissimilar in many respects. She was a Mother-goddess, one of a great number in the area. Gaia was said to have been the first. Then there were Rhea, Kybele, Demeter, Persephone, Kore, Ishtar, Isis, and others including Artemis. And since the East Mediterranean was a community, the identities of these individual goddesses sometimes became so merged that they became virtually indistinguishable. Herodotus equated Demeter

and Isis,[2] and also stated that Artemis was thought
by the Egyptians to be the daughter of Demeter,[3]
which would identify her with Persephone, the queen
of the underworld. Kybele, the Great Mother of
Phrygia, was often equated with Rhea, the Mother
of the gods. The identities of Artemis and Isis
became so assimilated that R.E. Witt calls the emergent
goddess the Great Isis-Artemis.[4] The problem of names
has never been satisfactorily resolved.

The function of these Mother-goddesses was always
the same. They were all Earth-Mothers, fertility
goddesses, who would become impregnated by the rains
from above. As Aechylus put it in his _Danaides_,
"The holy heaven yearns to wound (pierce) the earth,
and yearning layeth hold on the earth to join in
wedlock; the rain, fallen from the amorous heaven,
impregnates the earth, and it bringeth forth for
mankind the food of flocks and herds and Demeter's
gifts (corn) and from that moist marriage-rite the
woods put on their bloom. Of all things I am the
cause."[5] Although Aphrodite is speaking these words
in the play, the passage illustrates the concept
common of all Earth-Mothers: they were the generating
goddesses. Everything, including man, is now created
out of the earth. _Humus_, "earth," and _homo_, "man,"
have the same Latin roots. As Lucretius, a Roman
of the first century BC. stated, "Animals cannot
have fallen from the sky, nor the inhabitants of
earth have issued out of lagoons of salt water;
rightly has the earth been called 'Mother,' for out
of the earth all things have been created."[6]

It seemed natural to the worshippers of the
Earth-Mothers to link metaphorically and symbolically
the impregnating of the earth with the impregnating
of the human female. Thus the worship of the Earth-
Mothers involved human sexuality. In the worship
of Kybele, the Earth-Mother of Phrygia, men slashed
off their members and dashed them against the image
of the goddess, after which they were reverently
gathered and buried in the earth or in caves in the
earth.[7] Other rites required the priestesses of the
goddess to receive from the male ministers the means
of discharging their beneficent functions so that
the earth would be fruitful.[7] The sex orgies involved
in the worship of the Earth-Mothers are well docu-
mented. It should be added that the goddesses themselves were often the most promiscuous in the tales
related of them. One Great-Mother, Ishtar, was even
known as the "Prostitute."

John Chadwick comments on the important position held by Artemis in the area when he discusses her title potnia theron, Mistress, or Queen of the Wild Animals, showing linguistic evidence that the word potnia refers to an Earth-Mother. He explains that the word is often used of queens and is exactly matched by the Sanskrit patni. This shows that the word is of Indo-European origin and is not a prehellenic borrowing. But although the word is genuine Greek, Chadwick cautions, its use as a divine title may well be a translation of a pre-hellenic term of similar meaning, just as "Our Lady" is an English title familiar to Christians, and in other countries is translated by names of similar meaning.[8] Chadwick continues by referring to a newly-discovered tablet with a dedication "to the house of Potnia," and adds that in later times there was a district just outside Thebes called Potniai, "Ladies." "These Potniai," he states, "were understood by the classical Greeks as Demeter and her daughter, Persephone, who became Queen of Hades; that is to say, they continued in different aspects, the pre-hellenic cult of the Earth-Mother, which is so abundantly attested by figurines and pictures of all kinds throughout the Bronze Age. There can be no doubt that from early Helladic times onward, the cult of the Earth-Mother dominated religious life all over the Aegean world; and this continued into the classical period under a variety of names."[9] One of these names was Artemis of Ephesus.

However, the worship of the Ephesian Artemis was not limited to only the Aegean world but spread throughout the Mediterranean and perhaps even beyond. Strabo, for example, tells the story of how the Phoceans founded Massilia (Marseille). At the start of their journey, the Phoceans were directed to receive a guide from the Ephesian Artemis. Accordingly, some of the Phoceans put in at Ephesus and received from the deity a woman who went with them to become their chief priestess. They were also given some images, among which was one of Artemis and one of her temple so that they could build one at Massilia just like the one at Ephesus. The geographer also mentions temples of the Ephesian as far away as Iberia.[10] When Demetrius, the silversmith in the Book of Acts, boasted that Artemis was worshipped by all Asia and the world (19:27), he was not greatly exaggerating.

At this point it seems that for the sake of understanding and clarity, some chronological events and definitions are perhaps overdue. First, attention must focus on the island of Crete, which was a most significant link between countries in that part of the world. At about 1800 BC., a highly advanced civilization appeared on Crete as a result of waves of newcomers from the south, probably from the Nile delta region. This civilization, known to us as "Minoan" after the legendary King Minos,[11] continued there until about 1500 BC., when some catastrophe took place, possibly, but not surely, severe volcanic activity centered at the island of Thera. At any rate, a large part of the Minoan world was devastated, causing many of the inhabitants to leave for other parts, such as Greece, Asia Minor, the Levant, and Egypt.

Meanwhile, people from the north, of Indo-European stock, had made inroads into the Minoan world and from about 1450 BC. for several centuries became the dominant factor on Crete. These Indo-Europeans have become known to us as "Mycenaeans," although the term is regarded as a careless one. Because their chief city, Mycenae, was the first Bronze Age site identified in Greece, people today often use the term "Mycenaean" loosely to include practically all Indo-Europeans in the Aegean area at that time. These "Mycenaeans," who also occupied many other sites in Greece, the Aegean, Cyprus, Asia Minor, and the Levant, were known to the Hebrews as yewanim, corresponding etymologically to "Ionian." Their eponymous ancestor was Yawan, or "Javan" in the English Bible, the fourth son of Japheth, the son of Noah. Groups called "Ionians" later settled[12] along the coast of Asia Minor, including Ephesus. During the last half of the second millennium BC., the influence of these Mycenaeans was felt far abroad. Thus beginning about 1800 BC., Crete felt the impact of two movements, the earlier one from the Levant and the later one from the north which was ultimately to reach the Levant.

All this can be deduced because at the turn of the century, Sir Arthur Evans discovered at Knossos on Crete the palace of King Minos of Greek legend, and at the same time came upon three varieties of Minoan writing. The earliest form was pictographic; the next, chronologically,[13] Evans called Linear A; and the third, Linear B. These scripts remained undeciphered until in the early 1950's Michael Ventris identified the language belonging to Linear B as an early form of Greek.[14] Later Cyrus Gordon identified the language of the Linear A script as belonging

88

to the Semitic family, a language which the ancients would have called Phoenician. As Gordon tells us, while the dominant language of Crete thus changed, Minoan writing remained much the same; i.e., Linears A and B are related and were used in overlapping periods.[15]

The decipherment of Linear A allows us to infer that the Minoan civilization appeared on the island of Crete about 1800 BC. with an influx of people from the Levant. These newcomer, theorizes Gordon, came mainly from the Delta region, since their palaces, like those in Egypt, had no fixed hearths for heating during the raw, cold winters. Their Semitic language they brought with them. While it is not the purpose here to go into the decipherment of Linear A, one example might be cited to show the connection with Egypt. Quite a few personal names are Egyptian, ending in Re, originally the Egyptian sun-god: Ne-tu-ri-re, or "Re is divine."[16]

The identification of the language of the later Linear B script allows us to conclude that in some way the Linear A people had been displaced, at least in the important centers, by the Linear B Greeks, who became the ethnic factor on Crete between 1500 and 1400 BC. While the Mycenaeans undoubtedly had made their presence felt there prior to 1500, some catastrophe made the place uninhabitable to the Minoans and made it easier for the Mycenaeans to take over. Excavations on the island of Thera, which was the scene of two violent volcanic eruptions about this date, which perhaps were responsible for the destruction of the Minoan culture, show that the Minoan influence on the island was strong. Spyridon Marinatos the archaeologist there, speaks of great three-storeyed houses with unique wall paintings.[17] But after the Mycenaean culture was superimposed, it remained dominant until after the Trojan War. Perhaps this account will help to keep events in a time reference and also help to clarify the relationships of the different cultures.

The geographer Pausanias seems to have been much impressed by the antiquity of the city of Ephesus and the temple of the Ephesian Artemis there, noting that the cult of the Ephesian was far more ancient than the coming of the Ionians,[18] a fact borne out as already stated. The myth which he relates by its very nature takes things out of historical perspective and places them in the realm of the imagination. With apparent seriousness Pausanias maintains that the sanctuary of the Ephesian had been founded by Coresus, an aboriginal, and Ephesus was thought to have been a son of the river Cayster, from whom the city was named.[19] When the beginnings are lost in the dimness of the past, myth takes over.

The history of the neighboring city of Miletus is revealing. Pausanias states that the Milesians themselves gave him the account of their earliest history, that for two generations their land had been called Anactoria during the reign of Anax, an aboriginal, and of Asterius, his son. Then Miletus landed with a following of Cretans and appropriated the land, after which both the land and the city were named Miletus. Still at a later period, the Ionians arrived and captured the city, killing all the males they could find.[20] Thus if we read this account with our background of modern knowledge, we see that the Minoans arrived during the height of their civilization and took over from the aboriganals, but sometime probably subsequent to the beginning of the Linear B in Crete, the Mycenaeans arrived to overthrow the Minoans. These Indo-Europeans, settling along the coast of Asia Minor, then became known as "Ionians" and were referred to as such in the Biblical text.

Pausanias gave his version of the founding of Ephesus to refute another story that the city had been founded by the Amazons, women warriors who lived on the northern coast of Asia Minor. The Amazons were ruled by a queen, and the rest of their social system was strictly matriarchal. They were antagonistic toward men and put up with them only in inferior positions. To ensure the continuation of their race, according to some sources, they set aside an occasional time for a visit from males of a neighboring tribe. Other stories had the Amazons rely on chance encounters with strangers. At any rate, the female children were trained in the arts of war and in the hunt, while the male children were mutilated or killed, or perhaps taken back to the tribe of their father. Being trained in the arts of war and the hunt would naturally suggest the special patronage of Artemis, the virgin huntress of the Hellenes, but on the other hand, their treatment of the male children suggest the rites of the Great Mothers, as we shall see. And in spite of his scoffing at the story that the sanctuary of the Ephesian had been founded by the Amazons, Pausanias did admit

90

that some Amazons did dwell in the vicinity of the temple.[21]

In another passage Pausanias again speaks of the antiquity of Ephesus and the temple of Artemis, although he might seem to be inconsistent in what he says about the role of the Amazons: "All cities worship Artemis of Ephesus, and individuals hold her in honour above all the gods. The reason, in my view, is the renown of the Amazons, who traditionally dedicated the image, also the antiquity of this sanctuary. Three other points as well have contributed to her renown, the size of the temple, surpassing all buildings among men, the eminence of the city of the Ephesians and the renown of the goddess who dwells there."[22]

In spite of the inconsistency concerning the Amazons, there seems to have been no doubt in the mind of Pausanias of the great fame of the Ephesian and her temple and that they had been present long before the advent of the Greeks (Ionians). Artemis was a Great Mother whom the immigrating Indo-Europeans from the north must have found in every part of the Aegeo-Mediterranean area when they had first occupied the territory, and her cult must have contrasted sharply with the beliefs and customs with which they were familiar. Gilbert Murray comments on this situation when he speaks of "...the tradition of a Northern conquering race, organized on a patriarchal monogamous system vehemently distinct from the matrilinear customs of the Aegean or Hittite races, with their polygamy and polyandry, their agricultural rites, their sex-emblems and fertility goddesses. Contrast for a moment the sort of sexless Valkyrie who appears in the _Iliad_ under the name of Athena with the Kore of Ephesus, strangely called Artemis, a shapeless fertility figure with innumerable breasts.[23] The religion of the the Indo-Europeans never was able to supplant that found in the Aegeo-Mediterranean region. A compromise had to be made by a fusion.

This fertilty figure with innumerable breasts was preserved in the sanctuary of the great temple of Ephesus. The _Encyclopaedia Britannica_ informs us that the original statue was made of gold, ebony, silver and blackstone, the legs and hips covered by a garment decorated with reliefs of animals and _bees_. There was also a bee just above her feet.

The bee has always been accepted as an emblem

91

of the Ephesian, archaeology and numismatics bearing
out this association. The British Museum possesses
a collection of coins of the bee type, i.e., with
a figure of a bee on them. Some of the coins are
from Ephesus dating from before the sixth century
BC. to the third century BC. Coins from Crete, dating
from the fifth century BC. to the first century BC.
are also inscribed with bees. In the collection
also are coins from the Aegean islands, and finally
one from Troas (Troy). All these bee figures have
been identified with the Ephesian.

At Kamiros on the island of Rhodes, only a short
distance across the water from Ephesus, several
articles connected with the worship of Artemis have
been found. One is a series of seven gold plaques
on which is represented the winged figure of the
goddess with a lion on each side (the lion was also
associated with Artemis). Other gold plaques found
have the winged Artemis with the body of a bee, the
"Bee-goddess," as it has been called.[24]

Also, in a grave on the island of Thera, pieces
of jewelry have been found on which is depicted a
female head with a bee's body, similar to those found
at Kamiros. Hilda Ransome believes these also to
be connected with the worship of Artemis.[25] In addition,
some bronze objects have been found called _tesserae_,
which are not unlike coins and have been studied
by numismatists. These _tesserae_ depict the figure
of a bee on one side and a stag on the other, another
animal closely associated with Artemis. The figure
of the bee is enclosed within a mysterious inscription
which has been subject to various translations, but
Ransome is of the belief that it has something to
do with the secret rites of Artemis.[26]

The association of bees with deities in general,
and with Zeus in particular, has already been discussed, but the role the bee plays in the worship
of the Earth-Mothers is of special importance. Kybele,
the Great-Mother of Phrygia, was herself known as
"Queen-Bee" and her chief priestesses were still
being called _melissai_, bees, at the beginning of
the Christian era, the same probably holding true
for Artemis.[27] The priestesses of Demeter also were
known as bees, as were the women initiated into her
mysteries. After the arrival of Apollo at Delphi,
the chief oracle became known as the "Delphic bee"
and the priestesses as bees.[29] A word of caution concerning the term "Queen Bee" should be added here

to eliminate possible confusion. The Greeks and the Romans were patriarchal peoples, and being ignorant of the sex of bees, naturally called the leader of the hive "King-Bee." The Greek expression was Basileus ton melisson and the Greek, Apis rex. But for matriarchal peoples of the East Mediterranean who regarded their Great Mother as the chief deity, "Queen-Bee" would be quite proper. Modern translators, however, having the great knowledge of hindsight, render the term "Queen" regardless.

It is a good probability that not only the goddesses mentioned above were known as "Queen-Bees" but all the other Earth-Mothers as well, for they were linked metaphorically to the queen bees in nature in ways other than merely being leader of the hive or swarm. In nature, the male bee, or drone, is the one who necessarily must mate with the queen, but each of these chosen drones is destroyed, for their reproductive organs are torn away in the very act of fecundity. This fact in nature is reflected in the stories of these Mothers and also in certain ritualistic requirements such as their being served by eunuch priests. Take Kybele, for example. According to the story, this Great Mother had an affair with a handsome young boy by the name of Attis, who later broke faith with the goddess by having another affair with the nymph, Sagaritis. As a result, Attis went mad and castrated himself, "setting an example for the ministers of the goddess." [30] In other words, the ritual during which the male ministers of Kybele castrated themselves, flinging their members against the statue of the goddess, was in commemoration of the act of Attis. It was also emulating in a way the drone bee in nature.

This point is also made by Robert Graves, who cites stories of other goddesses to support his contention. He mentions the case of Aphrodite (also a Mother in some tales) and Anchises as well as Isis and Osiris. [31] In one story of Isis and Osiris, Graves notes that Osiris was castrated by the evil Set disguised as a wild boar. [32] Another tale of these two relates how Set killed Osiris, cutting up his body and scattering the pieces abroad. The grieving Isis was able to find all the pieces but the phallus. Still another story has Set throwing the phallus into the Nile. Isis, however, recovered it and, considering it worth divine honors, set up a likeness in the temple to be an object of esteem and reverence in the rites and sacrifices. Diodorus maintains

93

that the Greeks took this idea for the rites of Dionysos.[33] These variations in the tales all seem, however, to center on the one theme, the castration of Osiris and the importance of the phallus. Such was the case with the other Mothers.

Artemis as an Earth-Mother was also served by eunuch priests, called Megabyxoi, suggesting to W. K.C. Guthrie that originally Artemis, too, had had a youthful attendant and lover.[34] The term Megabyxoi is used by Herodotus several times as a proper noun, as a name for some Persians,[35] and there seems to be nothing in the name itself to suggest a eunuch. Thus when Strabo refers to the Megabyxoi as eunuch priests of Artemis,[36] there perhaps is a suggestion that their condition was man-made. At any rate, the geographer notes that the Megabyxoi were held in great honor and were continuously sought for abroad, although no reason was given.[37]

But the term Megabyxoi is worthy of further consideration. The Liddell and Scott Lexicon has the root of the word coming from bremetys, meaning "clamor" or "noise," and with the prefix mega, the meaning would thus be "great clamor" or "great noise." This meaning becomes of some significance in considering one story of the birth of the Ephesian. It will be recalled that in the story of the birth of Zeus on Crete, the Kouretes were present and made a great din, clashing cymbals, pounding drums, etc. while indulging in what was probably a fertility dance. This clamor that the Kouretes made, according to Callimachus in his Hymn to Zeus, was to prevent the infant's cries from being heard by his father, Kronos, who intended to devour all his children. The subject of these Kouretes is a complex and controversial one, but most scholars agree that they were fertility daemons, well-known on both Crete and Asia Minor, especially at Ephesus. At any rate, the following birth-story of Artemis (and Apollo) closely parallels the birth-story of the Cretan Zeus. According to Strabo, who relates the story,[38] Artemis and Apollo were born in Ortygia, a grove near Ephesus, which became so named after the nurse of the Ephesian. Above this grove was Mount Solmissos, where the Kouretes stationed themselves and raised a great din - this time not to distract Kronos but to frighten the jealous Hera, who was spying on the mother, Leto. The parallelism between the two stories is striking: both relate the story of a fertility deity, both include the Kouretes making a great clamor and performing a fertility dance. Zeus was fed by bees and Artemis took the bee as her symbol. As the name Megabyxoi means "great clamor," these priests correspond to the Kouretes of the birth-story of Zeus.

One other usage of the word megabyxoi may be of interest concerning Artemis. According to Liddell and Scott, megabyxoi logoi had the meaning of "boastings," literally a "great clamor of words." One is reminded of the great shout "Great is Artemis of the Ephesians" by the crowd at Ephesus, urged on by Demetrius, the silversmith, in their rage against St. Paul (Acts 19:23-28).

Some may think it curious that these Earth-Mothers sexually were so promiscuous, but one should remember that their function was fertility - of both mankind and nature. What is surprising, however, is that the Mothers were all regarded as virgins. One might well ask how a mother could also be a virgin, for these terms reflect a contradiction. The common explanation is that in those cultures "virgin" - parthenos in Greek and virgo in Latin - often meant just a young unwed girl, or perhaps a young wedded girl with no children. A virgin could even be a prostitute. Thus if one is aware of this fact, the explanation continues, the ambiguity disappears. To denote the meaning of "virgin as we use the term, to refer to a female with an unruptured hymen, the Romans used the expression virgo intacta. Christians have even used this explanation to account for the baby Jesus being born of a virgin mother. While some accept the Christian birth-story as a revelation of a miracle, others fall back on the above explanation that "virgin" means merely a young woman.

But the language of Matthew in the Greek New Testament hardly justifies either point of view. People of that time were not bothered by such a problem, for they were more than familiar with similar stories. The ancients were quite resourceful in explaining how their goddesses could have affairs, bear children and still retain their virginity. It was believed, for example, that the goddesses could have their virginity renewed periodically by a process of lustration. Pausanias relates that at Nauplia in the Peloponnesus there was a spring called Kanathos, and the Argives told him that each year Hera recovered her virginity by bathing in that spring.[39] Then there was the festival of the Athenian Plynteria, during which the statue of Athena was

bathed. Pausanias also tells of a temple of Artemis
at Corinth, in which the image of the goddess was
bathed by virgins.[41] Even Kybele, when her statue
was taken to Rome, was to be received only by chaste
hands, and was bathed by a priest in a purple robe.[42]
All these examples of the lustrations of goddesses
illustrate the same point; i.e., that parthenos and
virgo could refer to an "intact virgin" and often
did - otherwise there would be no point to a lustration which would renew the virginity of the goddess.

In the case of the Artemis of Greek myth, there
can be little doubt that she was regarded as an
"intact virgin." In fact one wonders how the Ephesian
Artemis ever survived the invasion of this hellenic
Artemis with her strict chastity and apparent enjoyment in killing both animals and humans with her
arrows. While Homer did at times refer to this
Artemis as "chaste," he mostly refers to the "archer"
Artemis, who used her weapon often and sometimes
cruelly. It may be of some significance, too, that
for divine persons, Homer reserves the word agnos[43]
meaning "pure," "chaste." or "holy" mostly for Artemis.
The Homeric Hymn to Artemis also sings of the "far-
shooting goddess who delights in arrows." And that
this Artemis is chaste, there is little doubt. Callimachus, in his Hymn to Artemis, relates how she
made the request of her father, Zeus, that she keep
her maidenhood forever (line 6). It is true that
the word parthenia is used here, but it is clear
that it is used to denote the state of an intact
virgin, for the writer later adds that none should
ever woo the maiden (line 264). As her request was
granted, it is impossible to understand how the goddess
could be anything except intact. Diodorus carries
on the tradition of the "chaste" Artemis, explaining
the importance of virginity in connection with oracles.
In ancient times, states Diodorus, virgins delivered
oracles because virgins have their natural innocence
intact and are in the same class as Artemis.[44]Certainly
Artemis was a virgin in the strictest sense of the
term and had little in common with Artemis the Earth-
Mother. Strangely enough, however, the Hellenes
also bestowed on the Archer the function of helping
women in childbirth. Perhaps it was this function
that helped bring together the two aspects of Artemis,
although some ambiguity may still exist.

Ironically, chastity and celibacy pervaded the
whole hierarchal system of the Ephesian Artemis,
perhaps suggesting the strong influence of the hellenic

goddess. The priests called <u>Megabyxoi</u> have already been noted as eunuchs, a state which requires celibacy. Also, the priestesses of Artemis, according to Strabo, were required to be <u>parthenoi</u> in order to serve as[45] colleagues of the Megabyxoi in their priestly office. In his article "Artemis" in the <u>Interpreter's Dictionary of the Bible</u>, F.W. Beare referred to these priestesses as "hierodules," but this is gravely misleading. Hieroduloi were temple slaves, prostitutes, most often associated with the worship of Aphrodite, especially at Corinth, where Strabo mentions them in the temple there.[46] But the priestesses at Ephesus were, just as Strabo said, <u>parthenoi</u>, strictly virgins. In addition, according to Callimachus in his Hymn to Artemis, the Ephesian was served by hand-maidens, nine-year old nymphs, "all maidens yet ungirdled." (line 14)

But what about the priests of Artemis called Essenes, the "king-bees" of the goddess? Pausanias introduces them when, in his description of the sanctuary of Artemis Hymnia at Orchomenos, states that the ministers there lived in purity, both sexually and otherwise, and that the corresponding priests of the Ephesian Artemis were called Essenes and lived in a similar fashion - but for a year only.[47] What happened after a year is not revealed. Perhaps the sentence had been shortened as a concession to the original Earth-Mother. At any rate, it is clear that chastity and celibacy were of prime importance in the worship of the Ephesian during the Roman period, an about-face from the worship of the Earth-Mother Artemis of earlier years except for the eunuch priests, vestigial remains of the ancient earth worship.

Perhaps the function performed by the Artemisian Essenes, King-bees, can be reconstructed. It is tempting, of course, to look for some metaphorical linking to the social structure of an actual bee hive, with Artemis as Queen Bee, the priestesses as melissai, and the Essenes as king-bees, or drones. But such a metaphorical linking cannot be made. In the first place, the ancients were quite ignorant as to the sex of the different kinds of bees. Aristotle, undoubtedly the greatest naturalist of the time, made an extensive study and classification of a good part of the animal kingdom. He referred to the queen bee of a swarm as <u>basileus ton melisson</u>,[48] "king of the bees." At other times he merely referred to her as <u>basileus</u>,"king" or <u>egemon</u>,"leader."[49] In commenting farther, he has the following to say about the drones and workers: "Nor is it reasonable to hold that 'bees' (melissai) are female and drones (kephenes) male; because Nature does not assign defensive weapons to any female creature; yet while drones are without a sting, all 'bees' have one. Nor is the converse view reasonable, that 'bees' are male and drones female, because no male creatures make a habit of taking trouble over their young, whereas in fact 'bees' do."[50] Since neither idea seemed reasonable to Aristotle, he concluded that bees (all kinds) generate without copulation[51] and that bees contain in themselves both the male and female "factor" just as plants do.[52] Other writers also show their ignorance concerning the sex of bees. Hesiod, for example, in one place metaphorically compares the idle man to the drone,[53] but in another place compares women to drones.[54] It is known, too, that as late as the Middle Ages the "Romishe Churche" was pictured as a bee-hive with the Pope in the position of "King-bee."[55] Such a drawing not only shows the continuing ignorance concerning the sex of bees but also suggests the continuing importance of the place of bees even in Christian theology.

But although the sex of bees remained unknown, names for them were not lacking. Why should the word essen be used to denote "king-bee" when the Greek vocabulary includes the words used by Aristotle, as already noted, especially basileus to refer to the chief of a hive or swarm? A possibility is that since the pre-hellenic peoples of the East Mediterranean had matriarchal societies, basileus obviously could not be used. Even the feminine basilissa would be inappropriate even if the gender of bees had been known. But these matriarchal people had to have some sort of "king-bee" to perform sexual or other duties, just as the Great Mothers had to have their consorts. Essen then becomes a possibility, as perhaps this word was suggested by esmos, "that which swarms, such as bees." (Liddell and Scott) It is interesting that Callimachus, who undoubtedly was aware of the matriarchal tradition, having lived in Egypt, is one who uses the word essen in this way and always in a religious context.[56]

At any rate, Pausanias can again be appealed to for help. The Essenes, states Pausanias, were istiatores of the Ephesian Artemis,[57] the translator of the Loeb edition rendering the meaning as "entertainers," including the quotation marks, making the meaning quite suggestive. But the root estia has to do with hospitality, and many words including the root have to do with feasting, banqueting, and entertainment. Estiao means "to entertain" or "to feast, while in the passive voice it means "to be a guest" or "to feast on." Thus Estiatores (the initial e is interchangeable with i depending on the dialect) were office bearers of a religious organization, priests, whose functions had to do with the festivals and banquets for the deity.

Before the arrival of the chaste Artemis of the Hellenes, the essenoi, or estiatores, of the Ephesian Artemis, being in charge of the feasts and banquets, could very well have been the male "entertainers," whose duties could have included sexual activities to ensure the fertility in Nature. Liddell and Scott's Lexicon indicates that estiatores and orgeones can be equated, the root of the latter being used in words such as orgao, meaning, in reference to men, to "swell with lust" or to "wax wanton." A related word is orgia, from which is derived "orgy," which originally meant secret rites used in connection with Demeter and Kybele and later with Dionysos. Thus when the newcomers came from the north, they used these words to identify the priests who were concerned with fertility rites.

But under the strong influence of the chaste Artemis of the newcomers, the rites and worship of the Ephesian became modified, and the sexual connotation of estiatores changed. The word estiator is related to Hestia, the virgin goddess of the sacred hearth, not only of the home, but of the town, temple, or federation, and the hearth was the symbol of hospitality. An estiator was one who gave a banquet, and at Athens was the one on whom the liturgy of the estasis fell, the public dinner given at a person's own expense to his fellow-citizens. The banquet might be given by a magistrate entering public life.[58] At Delphi, the estiator was the manager of the commissariat. Thus after some time had elapsed, the estiatores, or essenoi became stewards placed in charge of the liturgy connected with the feasts and festivals at the temple of the goddess of Ephesus, and were required, as Pausanias stated, to remain chaste for a year.

Let us turn back for a moment to the story concerning the birth of Artemis at the grove of Ortygia above Ephesus. The custom arose, as an observance of the occasion, to hold a general festival there annually. During this festival, relates Strabo, youths vied for honor, especially in the splendor of banquets.[59] The geographer also relates that a special college of the Kouretes held symposiums at the festival and performed certain mystic sacrifices.[60] It is not beyond the realm of possibility that the youths who prepared the banquests for the occasion were, or became, the priests called Essenes. They, perhaps, were given charge of the commissariat, while the Kouretes, as suggested above, became the Megabyxoi.

Since most people of the present day think of a commissary or a commissariat in connection with military service, it might be helpful to point out that according to the New International Dictionary, commissary is defined as "(1) One to whom is committed some charge, duty, or office by some superior power; (2) hence (Eccl.) an officer with spiritual or ecclesiastical jurisdiction as a representative of the bishop." These definitions allow the suggestion that the duties of the Artemisian Essenes were as commissaries of the temple: they were high priests representing a higher power, the Ephesian herself, by being in charge of the liturgy of official feasts and festivals, and might even have been the treasurers of the temple. They were "king-bees," subordinate only to the Queen-bee, Artemis.

Thus the picture of the Ephesian Artemis and her worship changed over a period of time. In the Bronze Age she had been one of the great Earth-Mothers of the area, whose function was to ensure the fertility of the earth and mankind. Then as the years passed, her contact with the chaste Hellenic Artemis altered the nature of her rites and worship. While she remained an Earth-Mother and promoted fertility, she was also a virgin, a phenomenon not uncommon for Earth-Goddesses. Her female attendants also were virgins, and her Megabyxoi priests remained celibate because they were eunuchs and had no choice, while the priestly Essenes, the king-bees, were required to remain celibate for a year. And so the Ephesian Artemis, the Queen-bee, and her priests the Essenes, the king-bees, were the principals of a religion which, if we can judge by the Book of Acts, more than rivalled Judaism and the early Christian movement as well. Each must have been affected by the other two.

NOTES FOR CHAPTER VI

1.   Homer, The Iliad. XXI.470.

2.   Herodotus, II.59.

3.   Ibid. II.156.

4.   Witt, Isis in the Graeco-Roman World, Chapter XII.

5.   Aeschylus, Fragments (Loeb Classical Library, Cambridge:Harvard, 1963) 25.

6.   Lucretius, On the Nature of Things, V.796 f.

7.   Sir James Frazer, The New Golden Bough. Theodor H. Gaster, ed. (New York:Criterion, 1959), p. 371.

8.   John Chadwick, The Mycenaean World (Cambridge: Cambridge University Press, 1976) p. 92.

9.   Ibid., p. 93.

10. Strabo 4.1.4.

11. The term Minoan is misleading as it is used at times to identify historical periods as far back as 2700 BC., predating by far the king of that name. It is possible, however, that "Minos" was a title rather than a name and thus may refer to a line of kings. In this study, Minoan is used for persons and things Cretan generally during the Bronze Age.

12. The terms Mycenaean and Ionian will be used when appropriate, but mostly Hellenes and Greeks will be used even though these names were not bestowed upon these Indo-European peoples until a later date.

13. Sir Arthur Evans, The Palace of Minos, Knossos (New York: Biblo and Tannen, 1964).

14. See Michael Ventris and John Chadwick, Documents in Mycenaean Greek (Cambridge, 1956); also John Chadwick, The Decipherment of Linear B (New York: Random House, 1958).

101

15. Cyrus H. Gordon, Evidence for the Minoan Language (Ventnor: Ventnor Publishers, 1966).

16. Ibid., Ugarit and Minoan Crete (New York: Norton, 1956), p. 30.

17. S. Marinatos and M. Hirmer, Krete, Thera, und das Mykenische Hellas, 2nd ed. (Munich, 1973).

18. Pausanias, Description of Greece, Book VII "Achaia" v.8.

19. Ibid.

20. Ibid., ii.6.

21. Ibid., ii.8.

22. Ibid., Book IV "Messenia" xxxi.8.

23. Gilbert Murray, The Five Stages of Greek Religion (Garden City: Doubleday, 3rd ed.) p. 56-57.

24. Ransome, The Sacred Bee, p. 60.

25. Ibid.

26. Ibid. p. 59-60.

27. Cook, Zeus I, p. 444.

28. Ibid., p. 443.

29. Ibid., p. 444-445.

30. Ovid, Fasti (Loeb Classical Library, Cambridge: Harvard, 1967) IV. 225-245.

31. Graves, Greek Myths, I, p. 71-72.

32. Ibid.

33. Diodorus, I.22.7.

34. Guthrie, The Greeks and Their Gods, p. 103.

35. See index of Herodotus (Loeb),

36. Strabo, 14.1.23.

37. Ibid.

38. Ibid., 1.20.

39. Pausanias Book II "Corinth" xxxviii.2.

40. Callimachus, "Bath of Pallas.

41. Pausanias Book II "Corinth, x.4.

42. Ovid., Fasti IV. 259-349.

43. Homer, The Odyssey V. 123 passim.

44. Diodorus, XVI.26.6.

45. Strabo, 14.1.23.

46. Ibid., 8.6.20.

47. Pausanias, Book VIII "Arcadia" xiii.1.

48. Aristotle, History of Animals IX. 40.623 b.

49. Ibid. IX. 40 passim. Also Generation of Animals, III.10 passim.

50. Ibid. Generation of Animals III.759 b.5.

51. Ibid. III.10.759 b.29.

52. Ibid. III.10.759 b. 30.

53. Hesiod, Works and Days. 304.

54. Ibid., Theogony. 594 f.

55. Ransome, The Sacred Bee, p. 150.

56. Callimachus, "Hymn to Zeus," 64-65; "Aetia"178.20.

57. Pausanias, Book VIII "Arcadia" xiii.1.

58. Aristotle, Politics 1321 a. 37.

59. Strabo, 14.1.20.

60. Ibid.

"Great is Artemis of the Ephesians!"(Acts 19:28)
This Mediterranean Mother-goddess, with her
many breasts to nurture nature and mankind,
gradually assimilated some of the qualities
attributed to the Hellenic deity.

CHAPTER VII

THE ESSENES AND THE END OF DAYS

From the foregoing a strange fact emerges. The Jewish sect was referred to as "Essenes" apparently only by those who spoke or wrote in Greek. This would, of course, include Hellenized Jews, and historians are aware that at the time there were many such, including Josephus and Philo, both Jews who wrote in Greek. Pliny, writing in Latin, got his cue from the Greek. Neither Hebrew nor Aramaic has a word which can be unquestionably identified as "Essene." Neither the Old nor the New Testament contains the name, and, as has already been stated, it is totally lacking in the Scrolls themselves. It is true, as Millar Burrows states, that there were "some references" to Essenes in rabbinic literature, [1] but the words found in rabbinic literature are those which some scholars suggest may stand for "Essenes." The word esah, for example is used. This is the term mentioned earlier (Chapter IV, p. 49), meaning "deliberative assembly" and considered by some reputable scholars as being the derivation of "Essene." But on the other hand, this etymology is questioned by others. Thus it must be repeated that there is no Hebrew or Aramaic word that can be unquestionably the derivation of "Essene."

There is no doubt, however, that the word was used in Greek to refer to both the Jewish sect and to the priests of the Ephesian Artemis. One very probable reason, mentioned earlier, that writers who communicated in Greek used the word essen to refer to the Jewish sect is that the term was a transliteration of the Hebrew hoshen (sometimes transliterated chosen into English), which was part of the priest's ephod having to do with prediction, or what some would term prophecy. There is also little doubt that Greek-speaking peoples used "Essenes" to refer to the priests of Artemis, her "king-bees." For the Jewish sect, the term originally must have been used in derision, and the question naturally arises as to what factors might have been responsible for Greek-speaking people, or those writing in Greek, to use the identical term to designate the priests of an East-Mediterranean goddess on one hand, and on the other, a Jewish group who regarded themselves as the Elect of a Chosen people. While certain implications have been present in this study, one might ask whether there are things more specific in possible relationships between the two groups in the minds of the people of that time.

To suggest possibilities, we must return to the catastrophic days of Herod the Great and the beginning of the Christian era. Although we have examined this period from the viewpoint of identifying the Zealots as Essenes, it is impossible to understand fully this period of time in Judea without knowing something of the concept of the End of Days. The Last Times, or the End of Days, had been anticipated as a time of great trials, suffering, and catastrophes for the Jewish people, at which time the Messiah, or Messiahs, would appear. Following this period of disasters, the Kingdom of God would be ushered in. How long this turmoil would last was not known, but with some ingenious computation from the text of the Book of Daniel, it was believed that it would begin at a time corresponding to about 46 BC. Daniel 9:24-29 contains a prophecy that the Last Times could be expected to begin seventy weeks after the commandment of Cyrus to rebuild Jerusalem. But it was later understood that this "seventy weeks" actually meant seventy weeks of years, bringing the expected time to about 46 BC., just prior to the reign of Herod. Thus during Herod's reign and following, there was an electric expectancy among the people. Too, it was the time the Messiah was expected, and so it may be understandable why both John the Baptist and Jesus were thought by some to be the Anointed One.

Hugh J. Schonfield, in a rather startling book, paints a graphic picture of the times: "... if it (the time) could be put on canvas, (it) would seem to be the work of a madman, or of a drug addict. A whole nation was in the grip of delerium. The king on this throne was a sick and gloomy tyrant. His embittered subjects feared and detested him to an extent that was almost maniacal. Religious fanatics fasted and prayed, and preached wrath and judgement. Obsessed with conviction that the Last Times had come, terror and superstition overcame all reason among the people. Self-recrimination accompanied messianic fervour. No wonder when Herod died all hell was let loose."[2] While at first the emotion was one of relief, soon there was complete chaos.

Soldiers and brigands plundered. On one pretext or another, different leaders took turns at setting themselves up as king and gathered a following for awhile, and during this time thousands were killed and crucified.

Thus to many, the End of Days had arrived. A great conflagration or war with the forces of Belial would ensue, after which there would be a time of judgment and a time of salvation would be ushered in, presided over by the King-Messiah of Israel, or in the belief of the Essenes, by two Messiahs, a Priestly-Messiah as well as the King-Messiah. For the layman it should be explained that although the word Xristos is the equivalent of the Hebrew Messiah, the Christian concept of Christ (Xristos) is in no way related to the Hebrew concept of the Messiah. The Jewish Messiah was human, a prophet, a "Teacher of Righteousness" who was to usher in the Golden Age, a concept derived from Deuteronomy 18:15-18: "The Lord your God will raise up for you a prophet like me from among you, from among your brethren - him you shall heed....I will raise up for them a prophet like you from among their brethren, and I will put words in his mouth, and he shall speak to them all that I command him."

One event which was to help usher in the Golden Age was a banquet, which was to be presided over by the Messiah, or Messiahs, a great Messianic feast. This time is opportune to consider the importance of feasting and food in the religion of the Jews. Since God is the creator of all things, so the thought goes, food to the Israelites was a divine gift. Moreover, since the Israelites were His chosen people, they would not lack for this divine gift, a concept made clear from the beginning. According to the Book of Genesis, the Lord God planted the Garden of Eden, placed man in it, and "made to grow every tree that is pleasant to the sight and good for food." (2:09) Then on their escape from Egypt, the wandering Hebrews in the wilderness were supplied by God with manna from heaven.(Ex. 16) Later, just before the conquest of Canaan, the gift of food and water was renewed: "For the Lord your God is bringing you unto a good land, a land of brooks and water, of fountain and springs, flowing forth in valleys and hills, a land of wheat and barley, of vines and fig trees and pomegranates, a land of olive trees and honey, a land in which you will eat bread without scarcity ...." (Deut. 8:07-09.

From the beginning food became a kind of bond between the Lord and the Israelites. On Mount Sinai, Moses, Aaron, and the elders beheld God and ate and drank (Ex. 24:09-11), and the consumption of food held a most significant spot in sacrifices and offerings to the Lord. In the early days of Israel, food offerings were probably thought to be eaten by Yahweh, and these offerings continued as long as did the Temple. The Israelites felt that they had come closer to the Lord when they returned to Him a portion of His gifts. The story of Cain and Abel, the two sons of Adam and Eve, is of interest in this matter. It will be remembered that Abel was a "keeper of sheep," while Cain was a tiller of the ground." During the course of time, Cain brought to the Lord "an offering of the fruit of the ground," and Abel brought the choice portions of the "first of his flock." For some reason the Lord had "regard" for Abel's offering, but no "regard" for Cain's. This preference by the Lord for Abel's offering stirred up strong anger and resentment in Cain against his brother, resulting in Cain's murder of Abel. While this story may represent the ancient conflict between the agricultural way of life and the nomadic, as some scholars believe, the story makes clear that offerings to Yahweh were to consist of the prime portions of meat.

The point is emphasized in the Law. The instructions given by Yahweh were that burnt offerings of lamb were to be offered daily, one in the morning and one in the evening. These offerings were to be continued throughout the generations and were to be administered by Aaron and his sons, comprising the priesthood. (Ex. 29:38-45) An important stipulation, however, was that no "unholy" burnt offering was to be made, "unholy presumably meaning "unauthorized" or "alien." This stipulation, then, was a prohibition against food, meat especially, from non-Israelites, for such food would not have been blessed." These meat offerings, it should be understood, were not made by individual families, but were to be made at the tabernacle, the precursor of the Temple, for the eating of meat was a relatively rare occurrence and always had a religious significance. For ordinary meals in the home, meat was not that plentiful and for the most part was reserved for special occasions, such as the arrival of an honored guest or the "return of a prodigal son." In those days, the offering of hospitality was a religious obligation. For example, in asserting his innocence of any sin,

Job cries that he has always offered hospitality, that no stranger had ever lodged in the street and that he, Job, had always opened his door to the traveler (31:32). The previous verse is more obscure, but apparently the men of Job's tent (or tabernacle) asked the rhetorical question as to who had not been filled by his (Job's) meat (31:31 RSV). Such a concept of hospitality was common throughout the whole region.

The Jews from ancient times have observed many festal occasions and feasts for which food and its preparation are most important. There are the "appointed feasts" such as the sabbath, the New Moon, the seventh year and the pentecostal year. Then there are the Pilgrim Feasts - Passover and the Feast of Unleavened Bread, the Feast of Weeks, and the Feast of Booths. There are also noncanonical feasts such as the Feast of Dedication and Purim.[3] The Zadokite Document relates that God revealed to the remnant, those who held fast to keep his commandments, where Israel had gone astray in the past, even in keeping "His holy sabbaths and His glorious festivals..."[4] This would seem to indicate that the Remnant, one of the names by which the Essenes referred to themselves, had maintained observances of these occasions in the past and would continue to do so in the future. Special care would be taken, of course, for the Messianic Feast at the End of Days.

Reference was made earlier to the expected Messiah as a prophet. The Essenes were deeply imbued with the spirit of the prophets, and many, if not all, of the prophets whose names have been given to Old Testament books are represented among the scrolls and fragments from the Qumran caves. In fact there are two scrolls of the Book of Isaiah, a prophet with whom the Essenes seemed to have felt a special kinship. The scrolls consist of two different versions of the book, the complete version called St. Mark's Isaiah Scroll, and one almost complete called the Hebrew University Scroll. Minor variations exist between the two.

A bit of the background of the prophet Isaiah may be useful at this point.[5] Following the death of Solomon, the united kingdom, for various reasons, became divided, the northern part becoming Israel and the southern part, Judah. Isaiah lived and prophesied in Judah mostly during the latter half of the eighth century BC. In that period of time the kingdom of Judah was threatened by four crises, and

Isaiah took an active part in the affairs of state. First, the allied kings of Israel and Damascus invaded Judah, after which these two powers were subjugated by the Assyrian Tiglath-Pileser III. Second, the northern kingdom of Israel was completely destroyed by Sargon II of Assyria. Third, either he or his son, Sennacherib, made a devastating raid upon Judah in 713-711 BC.; and fourth, Sennacharib made another raid in 701.

Isaiah's foreign policy during these crises consisted of trying to avoid entanglements with competing powers, and believed that Yahweh was using Assyria as "the rod of mine anger" (10:05) in order to punish Israel and Judah for straying from His path. But on the other hand, he believed that Yahweh would not suffer His Holy City to be destroyed. (31:05) In other words, while Isaiah was tireless in expounding his people's sins, he affirmed God's forgiveness and the restoration of some loved ones - the Remnant, as he called them. (10:21-22 f.) One of these passages seems to refer to the Essenes explicitly: "And the surviving remnant of the house of Judah shall again take root downward, and bear fruit upward; for out of Jerusalem shall go forth a remnant, and out of Mount Zion a band of survivors. The zeal of the Lord of hosts will accomplish this." (37:31-32) It should be noted that the term <u>zeal</u> is used in this passage. What Gaster calls a basic tenet of the Scrolls is the doctrine of the "Remnant," the belief that the community of the Scrolls constituted the true relic of Israel.

Another conviction of Isaiah was that the future would be under a "king in righteousness" (32:01), a righteous leader from "out of the stem of Jesse." (11:01) It has been assumed by many that this reference is to the Messiah, who would bring about on earth a reign of justice and peace. This expectation for the Messiah never diminished over the centuries, and it was at the time of the Essenes -the Remnant, the Elect - that the expectation became most acute and paved the way for Jesus to be accepted by some and rejected by others as the Messiah.

An interesting passage in Isaiah is the one which many consider to be the prophecy of the coming of the Messiah for the Jews or of the Christ for the Christians: "Therefore the Lord himself will give you a sign. Behold a virgin shall conceive and bear a son, and shall call his name Immanuel.

110

He shall eat butter and honey that he may know to refuse the evil and choose the good." (7:14-15) The Hebrew word <u>chemah</u> is rendered as "butter" in the King James Version and as "curds" in the American Revised, but the <u>Interpreter's Dictionary of the Bible</u> states that the modern equivalent is <u>leban</u>, which is prepared by churning fresh milk in a goat-skin containing leftover clots from the previous supply. (Under "Curds") Thus in spite of the variance in different translations, the reference is basically to milk and honey, and, as always, the two possess magical powers, this time to teach the coming Messiah the difference between good and evil. It would seem that those members of the Essenes who had been selected as beekeepers were performing not only a practical service but perhaps an eschatological one as well, caring for the source of the sacred honey for one who was thought by some to be the Messiah of Israel and later by others to be the Deity incarnate: "For unto us a child is born, unto us a child is given: and the government shall be upon his shoulder, and his name will be called Wonderful Counselor, Mighty God, Everlasting Father, Prince of Peace."

Another passage concerning honey, this time in Luke 24:41 f., also has to do with miraculous events in the life of Jesus. It is the time following the resurrection of Jesus when he appeared suddenly to his disciples. At first they disbelieved. But then he asked them, "Have ye any meat? And they gave him a piece of broiled fish and of an honeycomb." It is curious that "honeycomb" is included in the King James Version but omitted in the American Revised and other modern translations. The Greek and the Latin New Testament are not of much help. There is no mention of a honeycomb in the Greek, but the Latin includes it. Bible Commentaries are again of little help, merely noting that "honeycomb" was omitted by some ancient authorities. Any attempt at an answer is, of course, pure speculation, but were some of these "ancient authorities" aware of the pagan connotations regarding honey?

At any rate, let us return to the Essenes and the importance with which they regarded meals. Josephus informs us that the Essenes took two meals daily at the same time as other Jews. As laborers, they took their first meal at the fifth hour, after which they went back to their work. The other meal was in the evening, when any guest who in the meantime had put in an appearance would be invited to share the meal. This also was customary for Jews in general. But note the words used by Josephus to suggest a special piety on the part of the Essenes: (italics mine) "...after girding their loins, (the Essenes) bathe their bodies in cold water. After this <u>purification</u>, they assemble in a private apartment which <u>none of the uninitiated is permitted to enter</u>; <u>pure</u> now themselves, they repair to the refectory, as to some <u>sacred shrine</u>. When they have taken their seats in <u>silence</u>, the baker serves out the loaves to them in order, and the cook sets before each one a plate with a single course. Before meat the <u>priest</u> says a <u>grace</u>, and none may partake until after the <u>prayer</u>. When breakfast is ended, he pronounces a <u>further grace</u>; thus at the beginning and at the close, they <u>do homage to God as the bountiful giver of life</u>."[7] (It is a strange fact that the last clause written by Josephus concerning the piety of the Essenes toward their Lord could also be used by her followers to describe Artemis.) Josephus relates elsewhere that the meals were even prepared by priests.[8] It seems reasonable to infer that if Josephus, himself a Jew and one who had studied for admission to the Essene community, felt the need to comment about the piety of the Essenes toward their meals and their regard for the sacredness of the refectory, these rites must have been out of the ordinary. It seems remarkable that some scholars find no special meal of a clearly sacred character.[9]

Reference has been made earlier to the special Messianic banquet at the End of Days. One of the Qumran scrolls, often called the <u>Rule of the Congregation</u>, lays down the rules for this meal. The passage is translated by Burrows as follows: "And if they are met for the common table or to drink the wine, and the common table is set, and the wine is mixed for drinking, let not any put forth his hand on the first of the bread or the wine before the priest, for it is he who shall bless the first of the bread. And then the congregation of the community shall pronounce the blessing, each according to his rank. And according to this statute they shall do for every meal when they are met as many as ten men."[10] Dupont-Sommer maintains that "The present text (above) refers to the ideal Supper as it is to be celebrated at the end of time when the two Messiahs are present. But meanwhile, the daily supper in every community of at least ten members, with a priest presiding, draws its inspiration from this ideal liturgy of the messianic meal, of which

112

it is, as it were, both a reflection and an anticipation."[11]

Dupont-Sommer explains elsewhere what he means
by two Messiahs being present at the sacred supper.
He states that the priest mentioned is the Messiah
of Aaron - the Priest Messiah - the Teacher of Righteousness. He was a priest who had already come,
but it was believed by his followers that he would
return at the end of time, together with the Messiah
of Israel, the King-Messiah.[12] Thus, according to
the thinking of the Essenes, two Messiahs would be
present at the end of days, although it is possible
that as the thinking of the sect progressed, the
two Messiahs were merged into one.[13] Dupont-Sommer
is certain that this is what took place.

It is believed by some scholars that the Last
Supper was in reality a Jewish eschatological meal.
M.H. Shepherd states that "there can be no question
that the Supper was in Jesus' mind an anticipation
of the messianic banquets that he would share with
his disciples in the coming kingdom. The imagery
of the banquet was a common Jewish symbol for the
life of the age to come."[14] It is a matter of interest
that the thought has been entertained by some that
Jesus himself was an Essene, although such an eminent
scholar as Yigael Yadin argues against it.[15] But if
Jesus actually was an Essene, the Supper would have
been the usual Essenic meal, which in turn we have
seen to be thought of as a forerunner of the Messianic
meal at the end of days. Jesus, however, may have
regarded this particular supper with greater significance than the ordinary supper. The Disciples
apparently were to make preparations (Matt. 26:17;
Luke 22:7-9; Mark 14:12) and Jesus was to preside.
Jesus was also the first to touch the bread and wine,
an indication that he may very well have thought
himself to be a, or the, Messiah. The Supper can
be regarded, according to Shepherd, as a prayer of
the messianic community, or Essenes, that God remember
his Messiah by bringing into existence his kingdom.[16]

Upon examination, then, it would seem that the
Essenes of the Ephesian Artemis and the Jewish Essenes
performed similar functions, so to speak. The Artemisian Essenes were the commissaries for the feasts
and festivals of the goddess. The Jewish Essenes
were the Remnant in charge of the Messianic feast
at the end of days, of which each meal was a forerunner. They would also be responsible for feeding

the coming Immanuel sacred milk and honey and had
designated some of their members to superintend the
bees, which happened, ironically enough, to be the
symbol of the Ephesian. Is it beyond the realm of
possibility that Hellenistic-oriented Jews were able
to perceive a similarity in the role played by the
Artemisian Essenes on the one hand, and the Jewish
Essenes on the other in the preparation for, and
the observance of the festivals and feasts in the
worship of their respective Deities? Certainly the
opportunity was present for a derisive comparison
to be made.

Of course eschatology was an attractive field
for prophecy, for which the Essenes were so noted
and for which they owed much to the Graeco-Roman
world. Some of these eschatological prophecies are
found in the pseudepigraphic literature of the period.
Pseudepigrapha refers to a large group of writings
outside the Old Testament canon and the Apocrypha,
composed in Hebrew, Aramaic, and Greek between 200
BC. and 200 AD. The term itself refers to books
written by a person under a fictitious name, some
being attributed to Adam, Moses, and others. One
of these books is called the Sibylline Oracles, which
is really composed of 15 books in imitation of the
Sibylline Oracles of the Graeco-Roman world. Books
III, IV, and V are of Jewish origin, containing many
disconnected oracles about the Last Days, Book III
including many allusions to the final conflagration.
An interesting point is made by Gaster, who states
that while the book is a Jewish compilation dating
about 140 BC., the Jews seem to have adopted it from
Gentile sources, for it was held by Zeno and the
Stoics and dominated that part of the world from
the first century BC. to the third century AD.[17] The
fact that Zeno, the Stoic, was a Phoenician from
the island of Cyprus lends added interest because
of the location of the island, halfway between Judea
and Ephesus.

The eschatological doctrine that the world is
in the clutches of Belial, who ultimately will be
defeated is of course prominent in the Qumran scroll
commonly called "The War cf the Sons of Light and
the Sons of Darkness." But it is found too in the
Sibylline Oracles as well as in another book of the
Pseudepigrapha called "The Testament of Levi." Gaster
adds that the notion found in the War Scroll, that
angels too will fight, finds an echo in the Slavonic
Book of Enoch (17:01) where they are described as

the "armed troops of heaven," a play on the expression "heavenly hosts."[18] More will be said later about this apocalyptic war.

Jesus himself often prophesied about the End of Days. Matthew 24 is an interesting chapter in this respect. Here Jesus is prophesying what the conditions will be at the time, giving dire portents and warnings, cautioning especially about "false prophets" and "false messiahs." It is most startling that three times Jesus refers to the "Elect," one of the names used by the Essenes to identify themselves. The first time, he maintains that "...for the sake of the Elect those days (the days of great tribulation) will be shortened." (24:22) The second reference (24:24) is even more suggestive: "For false messiahs and false prophets will arise and show great signs and wonders, so as to lead astray, if possible, even the Elect." In the third reference Jesus seems to be speaking of angels when he uses the term (24:31): "And he will send out his angels with a loud trumpet call, and they will gather his Elect from the four winds, from one end of heaven to another." The fact that St. Paul uses the expression "elect angels" (I Tim. 5:21) supports the idea that Jesus is speaking of angels. Parallel passages to those in Matthew can be found in Mark's Gospel, 13:20; 13:22; 13:27. The question can be asked as to whether in the first two passages Jesus is referring to the Essenes. One must say that it makes sense, especially if Jesus himself was an Essene. Regardless, it looks as if he is prophesying that the Elect in Heaven, the angels, and the Elect on earth, the Essenes, would combine against the Sons of Darkness.

Another facet of Jewish eschatology was the doctrine that all things will be renewed, and is mentioned in a number of the hymns of the Qumran scrolls. Gaster points out that this doctrine is mentioned in a number of places in Jewish literature, the pseudepigraphic "Testament of Abraham" and the "Book of Jubilees" which speak of the renewal of the world after seven millenia. Gaster likewise informs us that it occurs in the very ancient form of the Jewish doxology, Kaddish, which is recited after a funeral, for God is there extolled as "He who will hereafter renew the world and quicken the dead."[19] Jesus also preached this doctrine of renewal: "And Jesus said unto them, Verily I say unto you, that ye which have followed me, in the regeneration when the Son of Man shall sit in the throne of his glory, ye also shall sit upon twelve thrones, judging the tribes of Israel." (Matt. 19:28)

In the last chapter it was shown that under the influence of the chaste Artemis of the Hellenes, the characteristics attributed to the Earth-Mother Artemis underwent significant changes over the years. From a fertility goddess with the usual fertility sexual rites and practices, a very gradual change took place so that while some of the outer observances seem to have remained the same, purity and chastity came to pervade the whole hierarchal system from Artemis down to the nine-year old maidens "yet un-girdled." The Megabyxoi had to remain chaste from necessity, while the Artemisian Essenes were required to be chaste for a year. The Jewish Essenes likewise eschewed women, another similarity which possibly contributed in part to their receiving the name "Essenes."

Jewish culture was strongly patriarchal. The prophets of Israel especially maintained the patri-archal imagery of God the "Father," and in the New Testament Jesus continually speaks of "Our Father" or "My Father." The instances are so numerous as to be banal. When, and if, the sect was given the name "Essenes" in scorn, the cry of Isaiah to his God could very well have been the cry of the Essenes: "Doubtless Thou art our Father though Abraham be ignorant of us and Israel acknowledges us not: Thou, O Lord, are our Father...." (Isaiah 63:16)

The result was that in this patriarchal society of Israel the interpretation of sex took the form, at least in part, of a reaction against all the fer-tility cults that surrounded Judea, including that of the Ephesian. The God of Israel, not the goddesses, is the source of fertility and fructification. Hosea makes this plain: "For she (Israel) does not know that it is I (the Lord) who gave her corn, new wine, and oil, I who lavished upon her silver and gold which they spent on the Baal. Therefore I will take back my corn at the harvest and my new wine at the vintage, and I will take away the wool and the flax which I gave her to cover her naked body..."(2:08-09)

In addition, man must curb his natural passions. IV Maccabees states clearly that the passions, includ-ing lust, are contrary to justice (1:03; 1:06), and justice, it will be remembered, was what the Essenes swore to uphold. To them, being temperate - in control

116

of the passions - was being just.(2:23) This book, IV Maccabees, claims that it is devoted entirely to a "philosophical proposition, namely, that religious reasoning is absolute master of the passions (1:1), a statement which sounds like something out of Plato. Reason counteracts lust. The writer cites Joseph as an example: "...the temperate Joseph is praised in that by reasoning, he subdued, on reflection, the indulgence of sense. For although young and ripe for sexual intercourse, he abrogated by reasoning the stimulus of his passions." (2:02-03) The reference, presumably, is to Joseph's encounter with Potipahr's wife. (Gen. 39:06-23)

Likewise, in the Book of Genesis we are told that the tree planted in the Garden of Eden grew the fruit which brought to man the knowledge of good and evil. While this tree is obviously allegorical, one interpretation is that it represents sexual knowledge, for the Qumran Scrolls state that knowing good and evil signifies the entire range of sexual experience.[20] And the woman for her disobedience was destined to have the man rule over her. (Gen.03:16)

But if the Hebrew system was a reaction to the fertility cults, their influence, nevertheless, was certainly felt by the Israelites, for there was every opportunity for both groups to learn from each other. As has been stated, Kybele's male devotees tried to achieve unity with her by castrating themselves, and her priests occupied her temples throughout Palestine - at Tyre, Joppa, Hierapolis, and even at Jerusalem.[21] The Israelites also had their cult prostitutes, sometimes women and at other times, men. In I Samuel 02:22 the temple prostitutes were women, while in II Kings they were men, called "sodomites" in the King James Version and "male cult prostitutes" in the Revised Standard Version. The term "sodomite" always referred to the male. Of course the prophets were continually reproaching the Israelites for such "rites." Hosea, for example, rails against harlotry and cult prostitutes (04:12-14), but cult prostitution was so extensive that Jeremiah inquires, "Lift up your eyes to the bare heights and see! Where have you not been lain with?" (03:02)

Some even see a connection between the fertility rite of castration and the Hebrew practice of circumcision. According to Genesis 17:09-14, Yahweh informed Abraham that circumcision was to be the sign of a covenant between Yahweh and his people throughout

117

the generations. Every male child was to undergo
this surgical ritual when eight days old. Yet it
is a well-known fact that circumcision did not orig-
inate with the Hebrews; the origin is lost in the
remoteness of antiquity. Herodotus claimed that
the Colchians, Egyptians, and Ethiopians were the
only nations that from the first had practiced circumcision, and that most other nations had learned from
the Egyptians.[22] It was an ancient custom, he explained.
But although the practice of circumcision was widespread in the ancient world, it may be of some significance that for the most part it was Semitic peoples
who followed the custom, and these peoples were
normally regarded as patriarchal.[23]

Among the theories concerning the significance
of circumcision, J.P. Hyatt lists three which he
believes deserve special mention.[24] The most interesting
for our purposes is that it was a form of sacrifice,
the sacrifice of reproductive powers to a fertility
deity. If such was the case with the Israelites,
they undoubtedly received the concept from neighboring
peoples, and the fact that blood must be shed with
the operation lends some support for the theory.
This theory, however, is rejected by many for a
variety of reasons, one being that the foreskin has
little to do with reproductive powers. During fertility rites, if the reproductive power was sacrificed,
the sacrifice consisted not only of the foreskin
but of the whole organ. Nevertheless, it is possible
that the foreskin was regarded as the symbol of the
whole organ - a part being offered in lieu of the
whole. It is possible, too, that at some time in
remote antiquity circumcision for the Hebrews may
indeed have been a representative sacrifice to the
tribal god, Yahweh, and that his followers would
thereafter be known by that sign. At any rate, the
importance of this covenant never diminished, and
when the Roman emperor, Hadrian, in the second century
AD. proclaimed an edict forbidding the practice,
the Jewish people rose in revolt. The prohibition
against circumcision was not the only catalyst but
it was an important one, and the Jews under their
messiah, Bar Kokhba, came close to defeating the
Roman Empire. But instead, it was the end of Judea.

In the letter of St. Paul to the Galatians there
is a passage which is most significant, 05:12. At
this point Paul was quite angry and made a bitterly
ironic comment about his adversaries, that is,
the members of what might be called the Judaizing party,

Jews who insisted that all converts be circumcised according to the Law, in this way opposing Paul, who allowed his Gentile converts to remain uncircumcised. Paul's attitude was that "neither circumcision counts for anything nor uncircumcision, but keeping the commandment of God." (I Cor. 07:19) This was a matter of major issue between the two groups and thus Paul's anger in his letter to the Galatians. In his letter, in referring to his adversaries, he submitted that those who had "unsettled" his Galatian brothers should "mutilate" themselves. In other words, Paul is making the sarcastic suggestion that those who were demanding that his Gentile converts be circumcised might well do a more thorough job by castrating themselves. The word for "mutilate" in the Greek text is apokopto, meaning "to cut off" or "to make oneself a eunuch." Such a suggestion would indeed strike a responsive chord with the Galatians, for Galatia was the territory of the great Mother-Goddess, Kybele, whose worshippers did castrate themselves during certain rites, as noted earlier. Artemis with her eunuch priests was also well-known in the territory. Scholars have long been aware that in making this statement, Paul is making the association with the Mother-Goddesses.[25] Also by making this suggestion, Paul may be implying that the idea behind circumcision is the substitution of the part for the whole.

Since the eunuch played such an important role in the fertility cults, and since most of the Jewish Essenes eschewed women, one might well ask whether castration may have been practiced by at least some of the Essenes, an act which of course would furnish further ammunition for their detractors. Such a question should not be ridiculed nor taken lightly, for the possibility is present.

The Law is quite explicit as to how the eunuch should be regarded: "He whose testicles are crushed or whose male member is cut off, shall not enter the assembly of the Lord." (Deut. 23:01) This part of the Law undoubtedly supplements the Lord's command to his newly-created male and female that they should be fruitful and multiply. (Gen. 01:28) Yet this statute seems to have become gradually modified over the years until the eunuch, if not wholly accepted, seems at least to warrant the Lord's blessing. The first voice of moderation is that of the prophet Isaiah, who is speaking for the Lord: "...and let not the eunuch say, 'Behold, I am a dry tree.'" Thus

119

says the Lord: To the eunuchs who keep my sabbaths, who choose the things that please me and hold fast my covenant, I will give in my house and within my walls a monument and a name which shall not be cut off." (Is. 56:03-05)

This passage is a most interesting one from a number of viewpoints. Jews find it difficult to accept the possibility that Isaiah was modifying the meaning of the Law. Thus the Jewish Encyclopedia states that the passage in question refers not to eunuchs "but as clear from the context, to persons who are impotent." Yet it must be confessed that the context does not make the point that clear. The Hebrew word in the Masoretic text for "eunuch" is saris, while in the Septuagint, the ancient Greek translation of the Old Testament and the Apochrypha, the word is eunokos. Granted that the word eunuch can be open to a few shades of meaning, it does not seem probable that the word in that context means a person who is merely impotent. However, this, too, will be open to examination.

But the most intriguing word in the Isaiah passage is the one meaning "to cut off," the Hebrew word karath. To begin with, the passage may be taken literally, that is, in spite of the eunuch's being physically unable to pass on his name to progeny, somehow, according to words attributed to the Lord, his name will be continued, not "cut off." But as is perfectly evident, a double entendre exists. What the Lord is saying here, according to Isaiah, is that the eunuch's name will not be cut off, even if his member is. And this double entendre is present in Hebrew as well as in English, for karath is used in both cases, for the name as well as the male member. For example, in the Isaiah passage above, it is used for the name's being cut off, but in the passage a little earlier, Deuteronomy 23:01, karath is used for the male member's being cut off. But the possibilities are not finished. Karath is also being used for the foreskin to be cut off in the case of circumcision, as can be read in Exodus 04:25, when Zipporah, the wife of Moses, took a stone and "cut off" the foreskin of her son and, by so doing, averted the wrath of Yahweh. Thus the theory is supported that in the rite, the part (foreskin) can symbolize the whole (male member), especially as Zipporah casts the foreskin at "his" feet, just as the worshippers of Kybele threw their castrated members at the feet of the goddess. It should be explained, however,

that the antecedent for "his" is not clear. In the
King James Version, the reference undoubtedly is
to the Lord, but in the Revised Standard Version,
the reference is to Moses, which is much more conven-
ient. But there is one more consideration: the word
karath also means "covenant" or "to make a covenant,"
although the latter expression is more often expressed
karath berith. Thus the Lord seems to be saying
through Isaiah something like this: "To the eunuchs
who keep my sabbaths and obey the rest of my Law,
since they cannot hold fast to my covenant as symbol-
ized by circumcision, the symbol that shall act as
a covenant is their cut-off member and their name
will be continued regardless." To this writer,
this sneaky double entendre is delightful, if a bit
grim, in a biblical text which otherwise is quite
devoid of humor.

The Apocryphal book of the Wisdom of Solomon
is another step in the continuum of the concept of
God's approval of eunuchs. The book is, as the title
suggests, ascribed to the venerated king, and although
it was actually written much later, the fact that
Solomon was given credit for its authorship points
to the suggestion that it should not be taken lightly.
The writer says, "Blessed is the eunuch, if he has
never done anything against the law and never harboured
a wicked thought against the Lord; he shall receive
special favor in return for his faith, and a place
in the Lord's temple to delight his heart the more."
(03:14) This is almost a paraphrase of the passage
in Isaiah.

In the world of the New Testament, the most
startling statement concerning eunuchs is credited
to Jesus himself. As they did on occasion, the
Pharisees were attempting to get Jesus unwittingly
to blaspheme the Law and were questioning him about
marriage when the subject of eunuchs came up. Jesus
stated, "For there are some eunuchs, which were born
so from their mother's womb; and there are some eunuchs, which were made eunuchs of men; and there
be eunuchs, which have made themselves eunuchs for
the kingdom of heaven's sake. He that is able to
receive it, let him receive it." (Matt. 19:12) If
Jesus was an Essene, a belief held by some, such
a statement would be construed by others as reflecting
the philosophy of the Essenes, thus supplying their
detractors with even further grounds for ridicule.

This rather shocking statement by Jesus has

been a most disturbing one for Christians, and for many years apologists have been explaining what they thought Jesus must have meant. The explanation that appeals to many is that his third classification is comprised of those who voluntarily give up, or repress, their reproductive powers "to better serve in the kingdom." Indeed this is the viewpoint of C.W. Wolf as he states it in his article "Eunuch" in the Interpreter's Dictionary of the Bible. The translators for the New English Bible also reflect this view, even to the extent of not even mentioning the word eunuch: "For while some are incapable of marriage because they were born so, or were made so by men, there are others who have themselves renounced marriage for the sake of the kingdom of Heaven. Let those accept it who can." Sensibilities seem to be offended by the use of "eunuch."

Early Christian theologians did not seem to be so concerned about the translation of Jesus' words, some of whom emascuated themselves voluntarily for the avoidance of sexual sin or temptation, accepting Jesus' words at face value. The most famous example was Origen, who performed the act of emasculating himself. Castration was also performed on themselves by some early Christian sects such as the third-century Valessi, who, not being satisfied with emasculating themselves, also performed their surgery on guests[26] in the belief that they were thereby serving God. It may be that these people were heeding not only Jesus' words found in Matt. 19:12, but also the words found in Matt. 5:30, which are somewhat less explicit than those of the former passage, but seem to underline the meaning nevertheless. These early Christans of course lived much closer to the time of Jesus than did the later apologists, and so there was less chance of misunderstanding.

Of the celibacy of the Essenes, or of the greater part of them, there is little doubt, and as stated, an argument can be made that it was the result of emasculation. Yet to those who gave the name "Essene" to the sect, it would make little difference whether such a practice existed or not. Celibacy was another seeming similarity between the Artemisian Essenes and the Jewish sect, which gave the detractors further opportunity for ridicule.

But the celibacy practiced by the Jewish Essenes was ironically for greatly different reasons. They practiced their continence for the sake of preparing to wage the war at the End of Days against Belial and the Sons of Darkness. They were following strictly the Levitical Law, for intercourse was considered to be polluting. (Lev. 15) thus any man who had copulated with his wife was considered unclean until evening. (Lev. 15:18) The Essenes believed that the End of Days was imminent and that they as "Volunteers" had to be prepared, and to be prepared, they had to follow the Law. According to the Law, the battle-camp was a holy place, for the Lord walked in the midst of the camp. (Deut. 23:14) Any sexual activity would make the place unholy, and the man would be banned from camp until evening after he had bathed. (Deut. 23:10-11; also Lev. 15:16-18) Thus married men were discouraged from entering the army, for continence had to be practiced if the Lord or His Messiah was to lead the Sons of Light into battle against the enemy. Also for the sake of continence any long-term enlistees were advised not to marry, and any newly-married man was charged not to go out with the Army. (Deut. 24:05) The Essenes, believing themselves to be the true Israel, sought to obey the Law strictly. The Qumran War Scroll emphasizes the required continence for the Essenes: "No toddling child or woman is to enter their camps from the moment they leave Jerusalem to go to war until they return.... Moreover, any man who is not yet cleansed from a bodily discharge on the day of the battle is not to go down with them; for heavenly angels march with their hosts."[27] Continence, then, was a most important requisite for fighting in the Army of the Lord against the Sons of Darkness. The Essenes shunned women, then, not because of some fertility rite, but to be eligible to fight as the Elect against the forces of Belial at the End of Days, which, during the days of Herod and later, they believed might be at hand.

The War Scroll also helps us to understand why the Essenes referred to themselves as the "Elect." As noted earlier, Gaster translated a passage as follows: "For with Thee in heaven are a multitude of holy beings, and armies of angels are in Thy holy abode, to serve as Thy legionnaires; and down on earth Thou hast likewise placed at Thy service the elect of an holy people."[28] Gaster has a footnote to this passage, explaining that the term elect also means "picked troops." Thus for the apocalyptic war against Belial and the Sons of Darkness, the Lord would head the Army with His Heavenly host of angels and on earth an army of "picked troops," the

Elect, the Essenes with their Messiah(s).

The apocalyptic war was to be, in the thinking of the Essenes, the ultimate crisis in the life of Israel. To win the war, the Israelites must follow the Law precisely, including the commandments concerning sexual purity at the time of battle. The war against the Romans must have seemed to the Essenes the War at the End of Days, especially with the destruction of the Temple. Yet they fought on. They were indeed picked troops.

So the Essenes thought of themselves as those mentioned by Isaiah, the Remnant of Israel, who prepared for the Day of the Lord by adhering precisely to the Law. They regarded themselves as the Elect, the Lord's picked troops on earth to match the picked troops of angels in heaven to fight the hordes of Belial. They kept themselves at constant readiness by remaining celibate as the Law prescribed for the troops of the faithful in their war against the hordes of Belial. Yet such practices by the Essenes were the very ones which the Hellenists of the region, including the many Hellenized Jews, saw in their distorted way as resembling practices followed by the priests of Artemis, the Great Mother of a neighboring religion. As a result, these Hellenists, then, bestowed upon this Jewish group the name by which the priests of Artemis were known: Essenes. Nothing could have been more ironically cruel at the moment, although effaced during the years.

NOTES FOR CHAPTER VII

1. Millar Burrows, The Dead Sea Scrolls (New York: Viking Press, 1955, p. 279.

2. Hugh J. Schonfield, The Passover Plot (Bantam ed. New York, 1967), p. 23.

3. For details see "Feasts and Fasts," The Interpreter's Dictionary of the Bible.

4. "The Zadokite Document" iii, 12-iv,6, Gaster, p. 64.

5. No distinction is made here between the First and Second Isaiah.

6. Gaster, p. 13.

7. Josephus II. 130-133.

8. Ibid.

9. Burrows, More Light on the Dead Sea Scrolls, p. 369.

10. Ibid., p. 71.

11. Dupont-Sommer, p. 109 n.

12. Ibid., p. 71.

13. Dupont-Sommer, The Jewish Sect of Qumran and the Essenes, trans. R.D. Barnett (New York: Macmillan Co., 1955), p. 5-6.

14. M.H. Shepherd, Jr., "Last Supper," The Interpreter's Dictionary of the Bible.

15. See Yigael Yadin, "The Temple Scroll," Biblical Archaeology Review,, Sept.-Oct, 1984, Vol. X, No.5.

16. M.H. Shepherd, Jr. "Last Supper," The Interpreter's Dictionary of the Bible.

17. Gaster, p. 22.

18. Ibid., p. 23.

19. _Ibid._, p. 23-24.

20. R. Gordis, "The Knowledge of Good and Evil in the Old Testament and the Qumran Scrolls," _Journal of Biblical Literature_ 76, 1957, p. 123-128.

21. Graves I, p. 117.

22. Herodotus II.104.

23. Robert Briffault, _The Mothers_ (New York: Grosset and Dunlap, 1963, Universal Edition), p. 80.

24. J.P. Hyatt, "Circumcision," _The Interpreter's Dictionary of the Bible_.

25. See _Abingdon Bible Commentary_; also A. Powell Davies, _The First Christian_ (New York: Farrar, Straus, and Company, 1957), p. 146.

26. "Eunuch," _Encyclopaedia Britannica_, 15th ed. (Chicago: William Benton Publisher, 1977).

27. Gaster, p. 290.

28. _Ibid._, p. 296.

128

fertility, 95.99,100,116, 117,118
festivals (see also feasts) 99,100,113
Florus, Gessius, 36
food, 79,107,108

Gaia, 85
Galatia(ns), 118,119
Galilee, 40
Garden of Eden, 107,117
Gaster, Theodor H., 2,10, 43,49,58,114,115,116
Gayley, Charles, 53
Gershom, family of, 13
God's Plantation, 2
Good and Evil, 111,114
Gordon, Cyrus H., 49,65,88, 89
Graves, Robert, 69,77,93
Great Mothers (see also Earth-Mothers), 90,91,93
Greeks, passim
Guthrie, W. K. C., 74

Habakkuk, Commentary on (Scroll), 38
Hades (see also after-life) 73,75,76
Hadrian, 77,118
Harrison, Jane, 66,67,70, 78,79
Hasideans, 19,28,29,31,32, 42
Hasmon(eans), 13,17,25,26, 27,29,30,31,32,35,37,38
hearth, 99
Hera, 94,95
Herod Agrippa, 36
Herod (The Great), 10,31, 35,37,38,60,61,106,123
Herodotus, 78,85,94,118
Hesiod, 75,76
Hestia (Vesta) (see also hearth), 99
Hierapolis, 117
Hippolytus, 2,3,4,5,10,12, 38,39,42
Hittites, 65,67,68,191

Homer, 70,73,75,76,77,78, 79.85,96
honey (honeycomb), Chapter V passim, 111,114
Honey tablets, 72
Honey Priestess(es), 77
Hosea, 116,117
h(c)oshen, 50,51,52,56,57, 58,59,61,65,105
hospitality (see also feasts), 99,108,109
Howlett, Duncan, 3,29
Hyatt, J. P., 118
Hyrcanus, John, 30,31

Iberia, 87
Ida, Mount, 75,76
Iliad, 70,75,91
Immanuel, 73,110,114
immortality (see after-life and soul
India, 67
Ionia(ns), 88,89,90,91
Isaiah, 57,109,110,116,119, 120,124
Ishtar (see also Earth-Mothers), 85,86
Isis (see also Earth-Mothers), 74,85,86,93
Israel (Northern Kingdom), 109,110
i(e)stiatores, 98,99

Jacob, Sons of, 51,58
Jannaeus, Alexander, 31
Japheth (son of Noah), 88
Javan (Yawan) (fourth son of Japheth), 88
jealous(y), 23,24,33
Jerome, St., 67
Jerusalem, passim
Jesus, 40,95,106,110,113, 115,121,122
Jesus, son of Ananias, 54
Job, 109
John, son of Mattathias, 26
John the Baptist, 106
Jonathan, son of Mattathias, 26,30,31,35

Jonathan, son of Saul, 52, 53,67
Joppa, 117
Joseph, 60,117
Josephus, Flavius, 2,3,4,5, 6,7,8,9,10,11,12,14,17, 20,22,28,31,35,36,37,38, 39,40,41,43,50,51,53,54, 56,57,59,60,61,105,112
Joshua, 43
Jubilees, 31,32
Jubilees, Book of, 115
Judah (Southern Kingdom), 109,110
Judaism, 1,3
Judas Aristobulus I, 30
Judas, the Essene, 59,60
Judas, the Galileean, 36,40
Judas Maccabeus, 26,28,29, 30,31,35
Judea, 35,54,65
Judgment, Time of, 107
Justice, sense of, 8,14,116

Kaddish, 115
Kamiros, 92
karath, 120-121
Kanathos, 95
kid (goat), 66
King-bee (see also bee and essen), 61,72,73,75,85, 93,97,98,100,105
Kingdom of God, 106
Kittim, 44
Knossos, 72
Kohath, family of, 13
Kore (see also Earth-Mothers),85
Kouretes, 75,76,94,100
Kybele (see also Earth-Mothers), 74,85,86,92, 93,96,99,117,120

lamb (see also offerings), 108
Last Days (see also End of Days), 43,106
Last Supper, 112,113
Leto, 94

Levi(tes), 19,23,24,37,55, 58
Levi, Testament of, 31
Linear A, 88,89
Linear B, 88,89,90
lion, associated with Artemis, 92
Lion of Wrath, 31
logion, 50,51,56
Lucretius, 86
lust (see also passions), 116,117
lustration, 95,96

Maccabees (see also Hasmoneans), 9,25,26,28,29, 30,42,43,117
Man of the Lie, 31
Manaemus (Menahem), 60,61
manna, 107
Manual of Discipline, 10, 13,19,58
Mariamne, 37
Marinatos, Spyridon, 89
marriage (see also women, celibacy), 8,9,121,122, 123
Masada, 1,2,28,35,36,40,41, 42,44,46
Masadah-Qumran, 41
Masoretic text, 73,120
Massilia (Marseille), 87
matriarchal systems, 90
Mattathias (Hasmon), 26,27, 28,30,36
Matthew, 95
Meals of the Essenes, 111, 112
meat (see also offerings), 108,109,111
Megabyxoi (priests of Artemis), 94,95,97,100,116
Meilikios, 78,79
Melchizedek, 58
Meli-genitor (Zeus), 77
Melissa, 77
Melissaios (Zeus), 77
melissai (see also bees), 92,93
Melisseus, 77

130

ABOUT THE AUTHOR

Dr. Allen H. Jones holds the rank of Professor Emeritus at Montgomery College in Rockville, Maryland. Retiring from that institution in 1973, he and his wife, Virginia, moved to Hilton Head Island, South Carolina in 1976. For many years his interest has been in comparative ideas in ancient East Mediterranean cultures, earning his doctorate in that field.

He and his wife, Virginia, have traveled and studied in many countries in the East Mediterranean area and were members of the archaeological expedition at Ashdod in Israel, the most important Philistine site ever excavated.

Dr. Jones is the author of Bronze Age Civilization: The Philistines and the Danites. He has also contributed to the Journal of Near Eastern Studies.